CW01456624

UNOFFICIAL

TAYLOR SWIFT

CROCHET

UNOFFICIAL

TAYLOR SWIFT

CROCHET

20+ PROJECTS

INSPIRED BY THE MUSIC AND STYLE ICON

Lee Sartori

QUARRY

Quarto.com

© 2024 Quarto Publishing Group USA Inc.
Text © 2024 Lee Sartori

First published in 2024 by Quarry Books, an imprint of The Quarto Group,
100 Cummings Center, Suite 265-D, Beverly, MA 01915, USA.
T (978) 282-9590 F (978) 283-2742

"Helpful Information" (pages 14–15) and "Crochet Techniques and Stitches"
(pages 127–140) previously published in *The Complete Photo Guide to Crochet,
2nd Edition*, by Margaret Hubert © 2014 Creative Publishing international.

All rights reserved. No part of this book may be reproduced in any form without written
permission of the copyright owners. All images in this book have been reproduced
with the knowledge and prior consent of the artists concerned, and no responsibility
is accepted by producer, publisher, or printer for any infringement of copyright or
otherwise, arising from the contents of this publication. Every effort has been made to
ensure that credits accurately comply with information supplied. We apologize for any
inaccuracies that may have occurred and will resolve inaccurate or missing information
in a subsequent reprinting of the book.

Quarry Books titles are also available at discount for retail, wholesale, promotional, and
bulk purchase. For details, contact the Special Sales Manager by email at specialsales@
quarto.com or by mail at The Quarto Group, Attn: Special Sales Manager, 100 Cummings
Center, Suite 265-D, Beverly, MA 01915, USA.

10 9 8 7 6 5 4 3 2 1

ISBN: 978-0-7603-9255-3

Digital edition published in 2024
eISBN: 978-0-7603-9256-0

Library of Congress Cataloging-in-Publication Data

Names: Sartori, Lee, author.
Title: Unofficial Taylor Swift crochet : 20+ projects inspired by the music
   and style icon / Lee Sartori.
Description: Beverly, MA, USA : Quarry, 2024. | Includes index.
Identifiers: LCCN 2024022662 (print) | LCCN 2024022663 (ebook) | ISBN
   9780760392553 (trade paperback) | ISBN 9780760392560 (ebook)
Subjects: LCSH: Crocheting--Patterns. | Swift, Taylor, 1989---Influence.
Classification: LCC TT820 .S2366 2024 (print) | LCC TT820 (ebook) | DDC
   746.43/4041--dc23/eng/20240603
LC record available at https://lccn.loc.gov/2024022662
LC ebook record available at https://lccn.loc.gov/2024022663

Crochet project designers: Hailey Bailey, Meghan Ballmer, Emily Davies,
   Julie Desjardins, Ashlee Elle, Krysten Grymes, Rachel Misner, Katy Petersen,
   Valérie Prieur-Côté, April Rongero, Lee Sartori, Wilma Westenberg

Design and page layout: Tanya Jacobson | tanyajacobson.co
Photography: Nicole Lapierre Photography | lapierrephotography.com
Cover illustration: Yann Legendre | yannlegendre.com
Fashion illustration: Emmanuela Di Maria | emmanueladimaria.it | @emmanuela_dimaria
Technical illustration: Kj Hay

Printed in China

This book is lovingly dedicated to my sister-in-law, Samantha, who always makes the whole place shimmer.

ACKNOWLEDGMENTS

I t takes a village to make a book, and I am so lucky to be surrounded by the best squad for this one! I would like to thank my friends who jumped in to help with some of the designs, Katy Petersen, Ashlee Elle, April Rongero, Meghan Ballmer, Rachel Misner, Emily Davies, Hailey Bailey, Wilma Westenberg, Valérie Prieur-Côté, Krysten Grymes, and Julie Desjardins. I would also like to thank the team at Lion Brand Yarn for their continued support of my work and the beautiful yarn for this project. I would like to thank my family, Sean, Noel, and Conan for coming on this journey of book writing with me for a fifth time. And lastly, I would love to thank my editor, Michelle Bredeson, who went quite literally above and beyond to make this experience absolutely wonderful. Michelle, you have a heart of pure gold, and I am so "enchanted" to have met you.

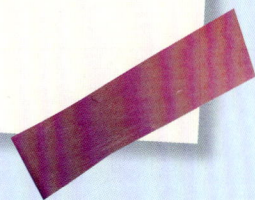

Contents

Chapter Four: Blossom, 96

PROJECT GALLERY

The projects in the book are organized by mood, and each chapter includes projects for a range of skill levels. This project gallery is organized by difficulty level, so you can quickly find the projects you want to make first!

Beginner
1 2 3 4

"Lover" Pillow
Page 23

"All Too Well" Scarf
Page 75

"Style" Newsboy Cap
Page 99

"Blank Space" Journal Cover
Page 109

"Bejeweled" Headband
Page 119

Easy

1 **2** 3 4

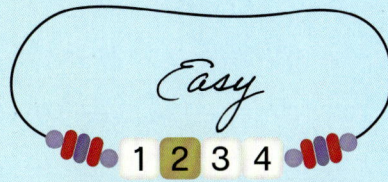

"Never Grow Up" Baby Blanket
Page 27

"Marjorie" Granny Square Blanket
Page 71

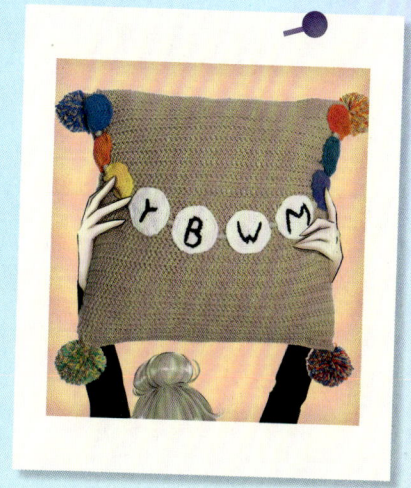

"You Belong with Me" Friendship
Bracelet Pillow
Page 99

"Wildest Dreams" Cardigan
Page 103

Reputation Taylor Doll
Page 113

"Fearless" Fingerless Gloves
Page 123

"Enchanted" Graphgan
Page 37

"Back to December" Hooded Cowl
Page 51

Evermore **Taylor Doll**
Page 55

"Shake It Off" Beanie
Page 81

"Karma" Cat Bag
Page 93

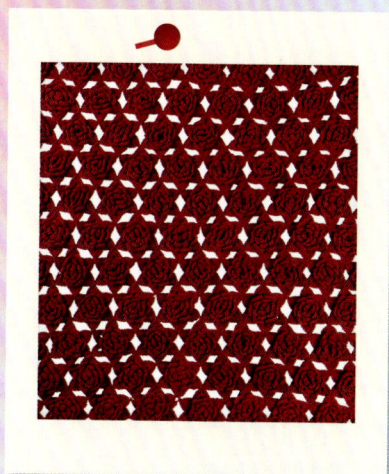

"Red" Roses Rug
Page 19

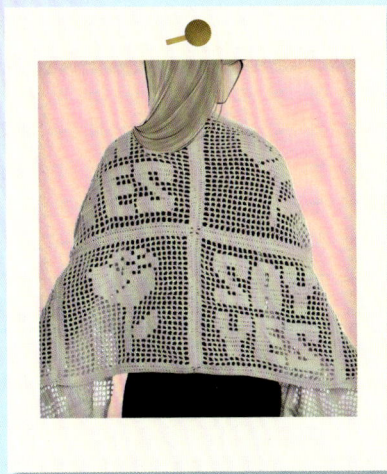

"Love Story" Wedding Shawl
Page 31

"Lavender Haze" Halter Top
Page 43

"Cardigan" Sweater
Page 63

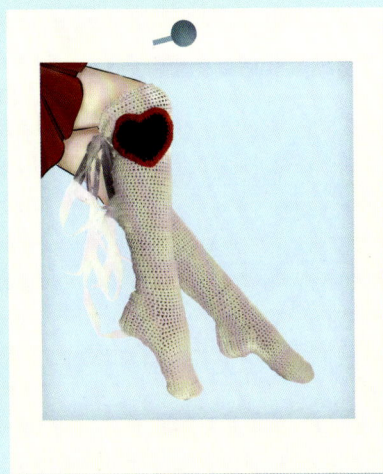

"22" Knee-High Socks
Page 85

INTRODUCTION

When I started writing this book, one of my favorite questions to ask people was, "When did you become a Swiftie?" The range is so interesting and amazing because it spans almost twenty years! Taylor Swift made her debut in 2006 with her self-titled album and started capturing hearts with songs like "Mary's Song." Two years later she backed it up with *Fearless*, and everyone remembers hearing "Love Story" playing absolutely everywhere they went. On *Speak Now* in 2010 we all became "Enchanted" with her even more. Then came *Red* in 2012 where our hearts broke for Taylor with songs like "All Too Well" (and we all needed a red scarf). In 2014 we had fun party vibes with *1989*, where we learned how to "Shake It Off."

There was some stress and anticipation when Taylor went dark for three years (the longest period between albums), but she returned with confidence and power with *Reputation* in 2017. We went back to the regular two-year wait for *Lover*, but it was worth it because we got "Cruel Summer." And then it was like Christmas for Swifties everywhere because Taylor gifted us two albums each year for almost every year to date. We got *Folklore* and its twin *Evermore* in 2020. We were gifted *Red (Taylor's Version)* in 2021 and *Midnights* in 2022. *Speak Now (Taylor's Version)* and *1989 (Taylor's Version)* came out in 2023, and as we worked on this book, the much-anticipated new album, *The Tortured Poets Department*, was released. It's been a journey, no matter what year you may have joined in.

It's an incredible body of work and it is AMAZING! Each album takes you on a rollercoaster of love, loss, joy, empowerment, and growth. There is a song for everyone, and from what I hear, everyone has a favorite. With these patterns, I hope we were able to capture some of the nostalgia and joy of Taylor's musical journey for you. It was hard to narrow it down to 21 crochet patterns because the possibilities are honestly endless. But from beginners to experienced crocheters, there is something here for everyone. I hope you see something that sparks joy for you! Happy crocheting, Swifties!

HELPFUL INFORMATION

Here are some things to keep in mind while stitching the patterns in this book. At the back of the book, you'll find a glossary of crochet stitches and techniques with photographs you can refer to if you're a beginner or are unfamiliar with a term.

Skill Levels

(1) Basic: Projects use basic stitches and may include increases and decreases.

(2) Easy: Projects may include simple stitch patterns, color work, and/or shaping.

(3) Intermediate: Projects may include involved stitch patterns, color work, and/or shaping.

(4) Complex: Projects may include complex stitch patterns, color work, and/or shaping, using a variety of techniques and stitches simultaneously.

Abbreviations

beg = beginning
BLO = back loop only
ch = chain
dc = double crochet
dc2tog = double crochet 2 stitches together
FLO = front loop only
hdc = half double crochet
rem = remain(ing)(s)
rep = repeat
rnd(s) = round(s)
RS = right side
sc = single crochet
sc2tog = single crochet 2 stitches together
sc3tog = single crochet 3 stitches together
sk = skip
sl st = slip stitch
st(s) = stitch(es)
tr = treble crochet
WS = wrong side
yo = yarn over

Term Conversions

Crochet techniques are the same universally, and everyone uses the same terms. However, US patterns and UK patterns are different because the terms denote different stitches. Here is a conversion chart to explain the differences.

US	UK
single crochet (sc)	double crochet (dc)
half double crochet (hdc)	half treble crochet (htr)
double crochet (dc)	treble crochet (tr)
treble crochet (tr)	double treble crochet (dtr)

Checking Your Gauge

Every pattern will tell you the exact yarn (or weight of yarn) to use, and what size hook to use to crochet an item with the same finished measurements as the project shown. It is important to choose yarn in the weight specified in order to successfully complete the project. The hook size recommended is the size an average crocheter would use to get the correct gauge. Gauge refers to the number of stitches and the number of rows in a given width and length, usually in 4" (10 cm) of crocheted fabric.

We can't all be average. Some of us crochet tighter, others looser. Before beginning to crochet a project, it is very important to take the time to check your gauge. Start by making a chain a little over 4" (10 cm) long, and then work the pattern stitch, using the yarn and hook called for in the instructions, until you have an approximate 4" (10 cm) square. Most crocheters do not get accurate row gauges because of the differences in how the stitch loop is picked up, so it is more accurate to check your gauge by the stitch count rather than row count.

The same flower crocheted with three consecutive hook sizes.

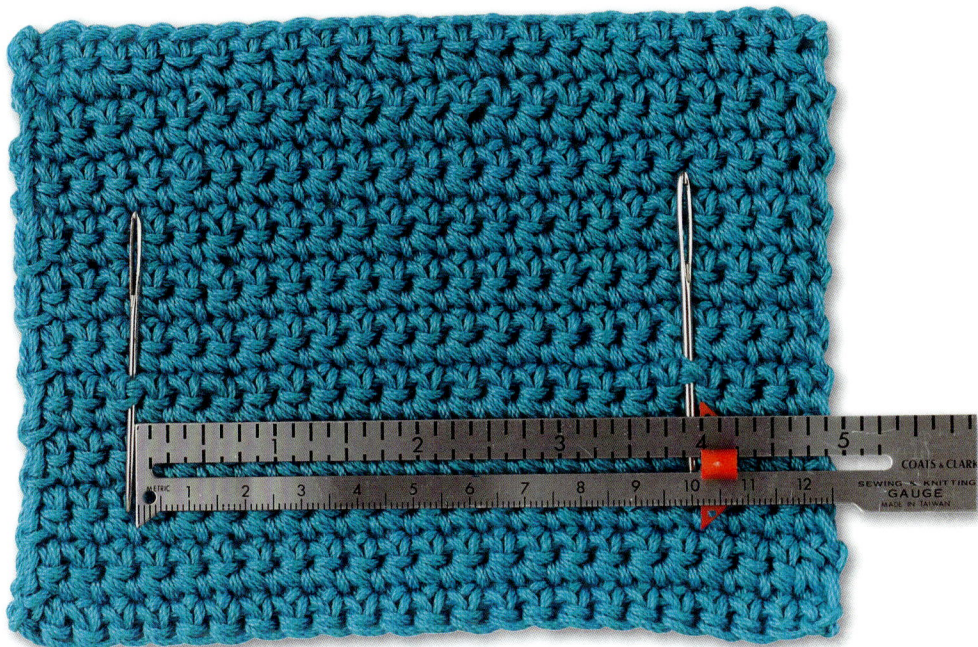

Place a pin on one side of the work and place another pin 4" (10 cm) over. Count the stitches between the pins. If you have more stitches to the inch than the instructions call for, you are working tighter than average; try a new swatch with a larger hook. If you have fewer stitches to the inch than the instructions call for, you are working looser than average; try a smaller hook.

Note

It is better to change hook size to get proper gauge, rather than trying to work tighter or looser. Usually the gauge stated means "as worked." In some instances, a pattern will give measurements of a garment "after blocking." This means that after an item is blocked it will stretch a little.

Hook Sizes

Metric Size	US Size
2.25 mm	B/1
2.75 mm	C/2
3.25 mm	D/3
3.5 mm	E/4
3.75 mm	F/5
4 mm	G/6
4.5 mm	7
5 mm	H/8
5.5 mm	I/9
6 mm	J/10
6.5 mm	K/10½
8 mm	L/11
9 mm	M/N/13
10 mm	N/P/15
15 mm	P/Q
16 mm	Q
19 mm	S

CHAPTER *One*

LOVE

Expressing love through crochet is one of the most beautiful things. Whether you're taking the time to crochet dozens of "Red" roses for a rug to give to a loved one or stitching up a baby blanket like the "Never Grow Up" pattern, each stitch you put into it exudes thoughtfulness and tenderness. The tales we tell through each and every "Love Story" is multifaceted and beautiful. I hope you enjoy all of the projects in this chapter, from the "Enchanted" Graphgan to the "Lover" Pillow, and my absolute favorite, the "Love Story" Wedding Shawl.

"Love is the one wild card."

—TAYLOR SWIFT

"Red is such an interesting color to correlate with emotion because it's on both ends of the spectrum. On one end you have happiness, falling in love, infatuation with someone, passion, all that. On the other end, you've got obsession, jealousy, danger, fear, anger and frustration."

—TAYLOR SWIFT

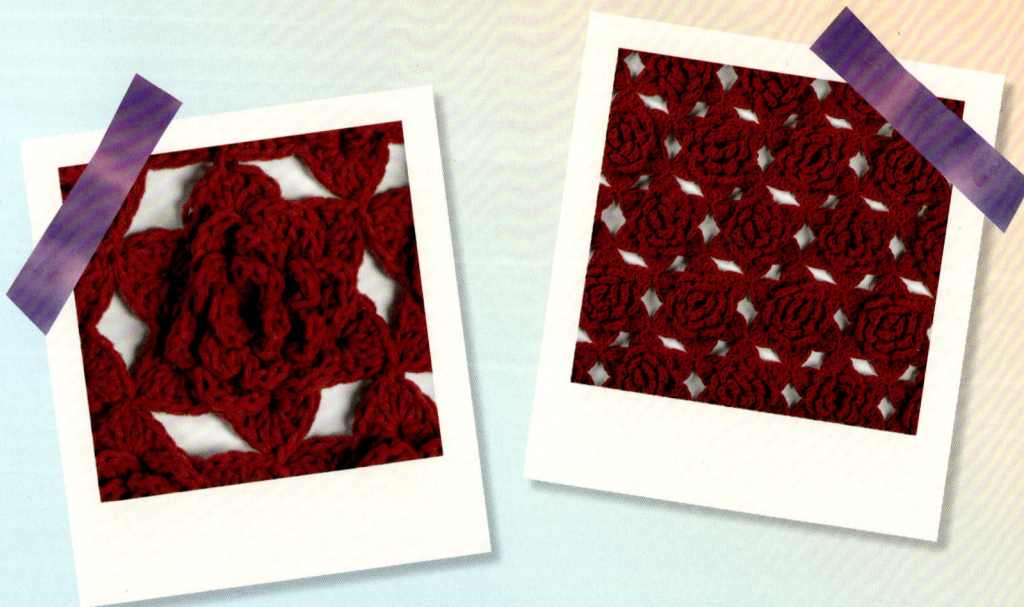

"Red" Roses Rug

1 2 3 **4**

Designed by Krysten Grymes

Love is such an emotional journey. It can be so passionate one second and end suddenly the next. These ups and downs and everything in between are what make love a whirlwind experience. It stays with you and peeks through in everyday moments, including when you settle in to do some crocheting. One of the beautiful things about working on something like a flower rug made of motifs is that as you are stitching, you can get caught up in the wistful memories of the past. It's a quiet time to reflect. As you are memorizing the repeats of the rose pattern, you are returning to the thoughts spinning around in your head.

The "Red" Roses Rug is made of individual flowers, each worked from the center outward and joined at the end of each round. The pattern for each rose is the same, so it's easy to memorize and very fun to make! The completed roses come together in one beautiful rug that holds all of the memories you brought with you along the way. The "Red" Roses Rug is the ideal way to stitch the autumn months away, so grab your intense red yarn and get ready to stitch up these roses one by one.

Measurements

50" x 60" (127 x 152.5 cm)

Yarn

Worsted weight (#4 Medium)

Shown here: Lion Brand Feels Like Butta, 218 yds (199 m), 3½ oz (100 g), 100% polyester: 18 balls 138 Cranberry

Hook

US size G/7 (4.5 mm) crochet hook. Adjust hook size if necessary to obtain correct gauge.

Notions

Yarn needle

Stitch marker

Scissors

Gauge

Each Flower is 4⅜" x 4⅜" (11 x 11 cm)

Notes

♥ Rug is made from 168 flowers. Petal points of flowers are joined together as the last round of each flower is worked, using a "join as you go" technique.

♥ Follow layout diagram for flower placement.

♥ Each flower is worked in continuous rounds.

Special Stitches

Magic Ring: Wrap yarn around two middle fingers from back to front, insert crochet hook under loop, yo and draw up a loop, yo and draw through loop (ch made). Continue with 1st round crochet instructions. Pull loop closed upon completion of 1st round crochet instructions. Secure end.

D

ONE: LOVE

19

FLOWER (MAKE 168)

Rnd 1: Make a magic ring, ch 1, work 6 sc into the ring. Pull beginning tail to cinch circle—6 sc.

Place a stitch marker in the front loop of the first st of Rnd 1. Place a 2nd stitch marker in the back loop of the first st. Move markers up as each rnd is worked to keep track of the front and back loops at the beginning of each rnd.

Rnd 2: Working in FLO of Rnd 1, *(hdc, 3 dc, hdc) in next st (petal made), sl st in next st; rep from * 2 more times—18 sts (3 petals).

Rnd 3: Working in BLO of Rnd 1, 2 hdc in each st—12 sts.

Rnd 4: Working in FLO of Rnd 3, *(hdc, 3 dc, hdc) in next st (petal made), sl st in next st; rep from * 5 more times—36 sts (6 petals).

Rnd 5: Working in BLO of Rnd 3, *3 hdc in next st, sk next st; rep from * 5 more times—18 sts.

Rnd 6: Working in FLO of Rnd 5, *(hdc, 2 dc) in next st (petal made), (2 dc, hdc) in next, sl st in next; rep from * 5 more times—42 sts (6 petals).

Rnd 7: Working in BLO of Rnd 5, *2 hdc in next st, hdc 2; rep from * 5 more times—24 sts.

In the next round, you will connect the point(s) of the flower to the points of neighboring flowers. Connect them using a "join as you go" method by making a sl st in the adjacent flower in the center stitch of the "7 dc" cluster.

FIRST FLOWER (NOT JOINED TO ANY OTHER FLOWERS)

Rnd 8: *7 dc in next st (petal made), sk next st, sl st in next st, sk next st; rep from * 5 more times—6 petals.

ALL REMAINING FLOWERS (JOIN-AS-YOU-GO TO NEIGHBORING FLOWER[S])

Before beginning Rnd 8, study the layout diagram and note the petals of the previous flowers that the current flower needs to be joined to. Work Rnd 8 AND each time you reach a petal that must be joined to a previous flower, work the petal as follows: 3 dc in next st of the flower you are currently making, sl st in point of petal of previous flower, 4 dc in same st of current flower, then continue working Rnd 8.

Continue to make and join flowers until all 168 flowers have been joined as shown in the layout diagram. You can join flowers in any order you like. To stay organized, we recommend joining flowers in rows, as indicated by the numbers on the first few rows of flowers of the layout diagram. Join 14 rows of 12 flowers each, as shown.

TAYLOR-MADE FOR YOU

For a fun nod to "Red," add a gray flower and a blue flower to capture each color reference included in the song.

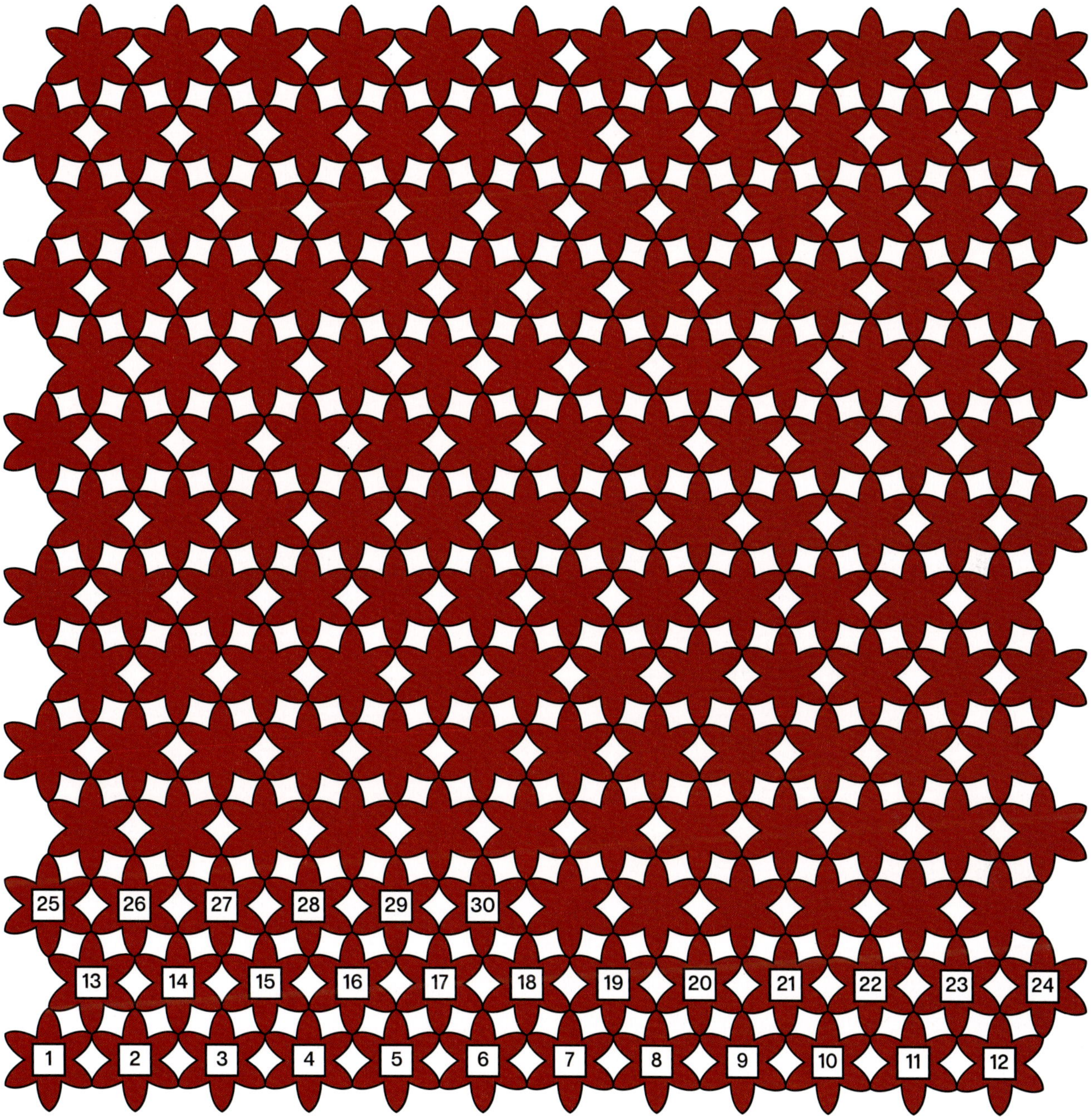
25
26
27
28
29
30
13
14
15
16
17
18
19
20
21
22
23
24
1
2
3
4
5
6
7
8
9
10
11
12

LAYOUT DIAGRAM

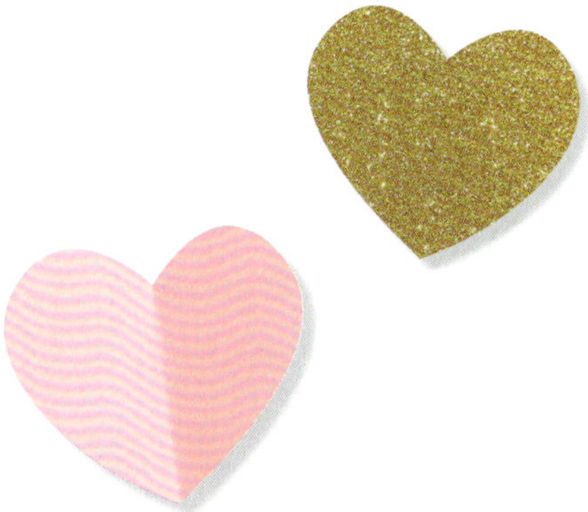

"I've been careful in love. I've been careless in love. And I've had adventures I wouldn't trade for anything."

—TAYLOR SWIFT

"Lover" Pillow

Designed by Lee Sartori

Even though Taylor Swift wrote "Lover" in 2019, this song absolutely sounds like it belongs at a wedding reception from the 1970s! It's so nostalgic and beautiful, a timeless confessional about the romantic and tender everyday moments we feel when we're in love. It makes us want to put on our best dress and our dancing shoes and waltz the night away on the dance floor with our family and friends.

The "Lover" Pillow is a nod to the Lover bodysuit that Taylor wears during her Eras Tour show, a glittery one-piece suit in the perfect pastel palette. The Eras Tour performances have become such an iconic connection to her songs, and the outfits Taylor wore in each set are no exception! With this pattern, you can crochet a cozy pillow that you'll want to take home and cuddle with forever and ever. And if your friends happen to stay over and crash in the living room, you might let them cuddle with it, too. Listen, it's your house and you make the rules!

Measurements

20" x 20" (51 x 51 cm)

Yarn

Worsted weight (#4 Medium)

Shown here: Lion Brand Lazy Days, 179 yds (164 m), 3½ oz (100 g), 100% polyester: 3 balls each 101 Cameo (A), 184 Peachy Pink (B); 2 balls each 105 Surf Spray (C), 107 Bluebell (D)

Hook

US size G/6 (4 mm) crochet hook. Adjust hook size if necessary to obtain correct gauge.

Notions

Large box [5 lb. (2.27 kg)] of fiberfill

Yarn needle

Stitch markers

Scissors

Gauge

26 sc x 28 rounds = 4" (10 cm)

Notes

♥ Pillow is worked from the top down by creating the tops of the hearts separately and then joining them for the remainder of the body of the pillow.

♥ Ensure that your pillow is the correct shape by stuffing it very firmly.

♥ Lettering is added at the end.

Special Stitches

Fdc (foundation double crochet): Ch 2, yo and insert hook in 2nd ch from hook, yo and pull up loop, yo and pull through 1 loop on hook (1st ch made), [yo and pull through 2 loops on hook] twice (dc made), *yo and insert hook into ch of previous foundation stitch, yo and pull up loop, yo and pull through 1 loop on hook (ch made), [yo and pull through 2 loops on hook] twice (dc made); rep from * until desired number of Fdc have been made.

inv-dec (invisible single crochet decrease): Insert hook in front loop only of each of next 2 sts, yarn over and draw through both sts, yarn over and draw through 2 loops on hook—1 st decreased.

CONTINUED

TAYLOR-MADE FOR YOU

Add some sew-on sequins or gems to make your pillow sparkle just like the "Lover" bodysuit!

TOP OF HEART (MAKE 2)

With A.

Rnd 1: Ch 2, 6 sc in 2nd ch from hook—6 sc.

Place marker in last sc made to indicate end of rnd. Move marker up as each rnd is completed.

Rnd 2: 2 sc in each st around—12 sc.

Rnd 3: [2 sc, sc in next st] around—18 sc.

Rnd 4: [Sc, 2 sc in next st, sc] around—24 sc.

Rnd 5: [2 sc, sc 3] around—30 sc.

Rnd 6: [Sc 2, 2 sc in next st, sc 2] around—36 sc.

Rnd 7: [2 sc, sc 5] around—42 sc.

Rnd 8: [Sc 3, 2 sc in next st, sc 3] around—48 sc.

Rnd 9: [2 sc, sc 7] around—54 sc.

Rnd 10: [Sc 4, 2 sc in next st, sc 4] around—60 sc.

Rnd 11: [2 sc, sc 9] around—66 sc.

Rnd 12: [Sc 5, 2 sc in next st, sc 5] around—72 sc.

Rnd 13: [2 sc, sc 11] around—78 sc.

Rnd 14: [Sc 6, 2 sc in next st, sc 6] around—84 sc.

Rnd 15: [2 sc, sc 13] around—90 sc.

Rnd 16: [Sc 7, 2 sc in next st, sc 7] around—96 sc.

Rnd 17: [2 sc, sc 15] around—102 sc.

Rnd 18: [Sc 8, 2 sc in next st, sc 8] around—108 sc.

Rnd 19: [2 sc, sc 17] around—114 sc.

Rnd 20: [Sc 9, 2 sc in next st, sc 9] around—120 sc.

Rnd 21: [2 sc, sc 19] around—126 sc.

Rnd 22: [Sc 10, 2 sc in next st, sc 10] around—132 sc.

Rnd 23: [2 sc, sc 21] around—138 sc.

Rnd 24: [Sc 11, 2 sc in next st, sc 11] around—144 sc.

Rnd 25: [2 sc, sc 23] around—150 sc.

Rnd 26: [Sc 12, 2 sc in next st, sc 12] around—156 sc.

Rnd 27: [2 sc, sc 25] around—162 sc.

Rnd 28: [Sc 13, 2 sc in next st, sc 13] around—168 sc.

Rnd 29: [2 sc, sc 27] around—174 sc.

Rnd 30: [Sc 14, 2 sc in next st, sc 14] around—180 sc.

Rnds 31–35: Sc around—180 sc.

Fasten off 1st piece and set aside. Do not fasten off 2nd piece. Continue to Body.

BODY

With A.

Rnd 1: Sc around 1st piece, hold 2nd piece in line with 1st and sc around 2nd piece—360 sc.

Change to B.

Rnd 2: Sc around—360 sc.

Rnd 3: [Sc 58, inv-dec, place a marker in decrease just made] 5 times, sc to last 2 sts, inv-dec—354 sc.

Rnd 4: Sc around.

Rnd 5: [Sc in each st to 1 st before next marked st, inv-dec, move marker to decrease just made] 5 times, sc in each st to last 2 sts, inv-dec—348 sc.

Rnd 6: Sc around.

Rnds 7–120: Rep Rnds 5 and 6, decreasing 6 sts every other rnd, until only 6 sts rem.

Change to C after Rnd 37, and D after Rnd 74. Stuff pillow before opening becomes too small.

Fasten off, weave in ends.

LETTERING

With A.

Row 1: Fdc 210.

Fasten off, leaving a long tail for sewing.

FINISHING

Using photo as a guide, pin your Lettering into the word Lover and tack it down by sewing or preferred method. Weave in ends.

Add stars by using lengths of all colors and sewing lines on the surface of the pillow.

"I still have mixed feelings about what growing up is—this thing that happens to everyone, so I've heard."

—TAYLOR SWIFT

"Never Grow Up" Baby Blanket

Designed by Katy Petersen

I had so many dreams for my babies when they were born; I think all parents do! As soon as I looked into each little face, I remember feeling fiercely protective and absolutely in love. I looked at their little eyelashes and their tiny fingers and held their soft baby hands and knew that this time was precious and fleeting. I also remember decorating their adorable little bedrooms with things that I knew they would like, like fuzzy toys and soft blankets. I also made each of them handmade blankets that they could keep as they grew older, a memento of how much the time we spent together meant to me. I dreamed that their blankets would be with them on their journey through life and how sweet it would be if someday they could share their blanket with a little one of their own.

Whether you are crocheting your "Never Grow Up" baby blanket for a little one of your own or as a special gift, you'll fall in love with the different textures and stitches in this pattern. This blanket is made of two different crochet stitch textures—the cluster stitch, and the crossed double crochet stitch. After making each of the squares, you'll join them together and add a beautiful border. The crochet textures are so lush and gorgeous, perfect for cuddling up or tucking in a little one for a cozy nap.

Measurements

36" x 36" (91.5 x 91.5 cm)

Yarn

Worsted weight (#4 Medium)

Shown here: Lion Brand Basic Stitch Anti-Microbial, 186 yds (170 m), 3½ oz (100 g), 65% recycled polyester, 35% Amicor acrylic: 7 balls 135 Spice

Hook

US size H/8 (5 mm) crochet hook. Adjust hook size if necessary to obtain correct gauge.

Notions

Yarn needle

Stitch marker

Scissors

Gauge

One square = 11" x 11" (28 x 28 cm)

Notes

♥ This blanket is made up of 9 large squares, including 5 of Square 1 and 4 of Square 2. The Squares are sewn together and a border is worked around the outer edge of the blanket.

♥ Square 1 is worked in rows of (sc, 2 dc).

♥ Square 2 is worked in alternating rows of CL and crossed dc; crossed dc sts are worked in the ch-2 spaces on either side of the CL sts and CL sts are worked in the space between the two dc of the crossed dc sts.

Special Stitches

Crossed dc: Sk next ch-2 space and CL, dc in next ch-2 space, working in front of the dc just made, dc in the skipped ch-2 space.

CL (Cluster): (Yo, insert hook in indicated space, pull up a loop) 3 times, yo, pull through all 7 loops on hook.

CONTINUED

SQUARE 1 (MAKE 5)

Ch 38.

Row 1 (RS): (Sc, 2 dc) in the 2nd ch from hook, sk 2 ch, *(sc, 2 dc) in next ch, sk 2 ch; rep from * across, sc in the last ch, turn—13 sc, 24 dc.

Rows 2–27: Ch 1, (sc, 2 dc) in the 1st sc, sk 2 dc, *(sc, 2 dc) in next sc, sk 2 dc; rep from * across, sc in the last sc, turn.

TAYLOR-MADE FOR YOU

Make your blanket unique by making each square a different color!

SQUARE 1 TRIM

Rnd 1: Ch 1, (sc, ch 2, sc) in the 1st sc, sc in next 35 sts, (sc, ch 2, sc) in the last sc, rotate square 90 degrees, evenly sc 35 times across edge to next corner, *(sc, ch 2, sc) in corner, rotate square 90 degrees, evenly sc 35 times across edge to next corner: rep from * once more, join with a sl stitch to the first sc—148 sc, 4 ch-2 spaces.

Rnd 2: Ch 1, sc in the 1st sc, (sc, ch 2, sc) in corner ch-2 space, *sc in each sc to next corner ch-2 space, (sc, ch 2, sc) in corner ch-2 space; rep from * 2 more times, sc in each remaining sc, join with a slip st to the 1st sc—156 sc, 4 ch-2 spaces.

Fasten off.

SQUARE 2 (MAKE 4)

Ch 36.

Row 1 (RS): Dc in the 5th ch from hook (4 sk ch count as a base ch and dc), working in front of the dc just made, dc in the last ch sk (crossed dc made), dc in next ch, *sk 1 ch, dc in next ch, working in front of the dc just made, dc in the sk ch, dc in next ch; rep from * across, turn—12 dc, 11 crossed dc.

Row 2 (WS): Ch 1, sc in the 1st dc, *ch 2, CL between the 2 crossed dc, ch 2, sk 2nd dc of the crossed dc, sc in next dc; rep from * across, turn—12 sc, 22 ch-2 spaces, 11 CL.

Row 3: Ch 3 (counts as a dc), *crossed dc in the ch-2 spaces on either side of the CL st, dc in next sc; rep from * across, turn—12 dc, 11 crossed dc.

Rows 4–21: Rep Rows 2 and 3.

SQUARE 2 TRIM

Rnd 1: Ch 1, (sc, ch 2, sc) in the 1st st, (sc in next 7 sts, 2 dc in next st) 3 times, sc in next 8 sts, (sc, ch 2, sc) in last st, rotate square 90 degrees, evenly sc 35 times across, *(sc, ch 2, sc) in corner, rotate square 90 degrees, evenly sc 35 times across: rep from * once more, join with a sl st to the 1st sc—148 sc, 4 ch-2 spaces.

Rnd 2: Ch 1, sc in the 1st sc, (sc, ch 2, sc) in corner ch-2 space, *sc in each sc to next corner ch-2 space, (sc, ch 2, sc) in corner ch-2 space; rep from * 2 more times, sc in each remaining sc, join with a sl st to the 1st sc—156 sc, 4 ch-2 spaces.

Fasten off.

ASSEMBLY

Using preferred method, sew squares together according to the diagram.

BORDER

Rnd 1: With RS facing, join to any corner ch-2 space, ch 1, *(sc, ch 2, sc) in corner ch-2 space, sc in each sc (skipping the ch-2 spaces and seams between squares) to next corner ch-2 space; rep from * 3 more times, join with a sl st to the 1st sc—476 sc, 4 ch-2 spaces.

Rnd 2: Ch 1, sc in the 1st sc, (sc, ch 2, sc) in corner ch-2 space, *sc in each sc to next corner ch-2 space, (sc, ch 2, sc) in corner ch-2 space; rep from * 2 more times, sc in each remaining sc, join with a sl st to the 1st sc—484 sc, 4 ch-2 spaces.

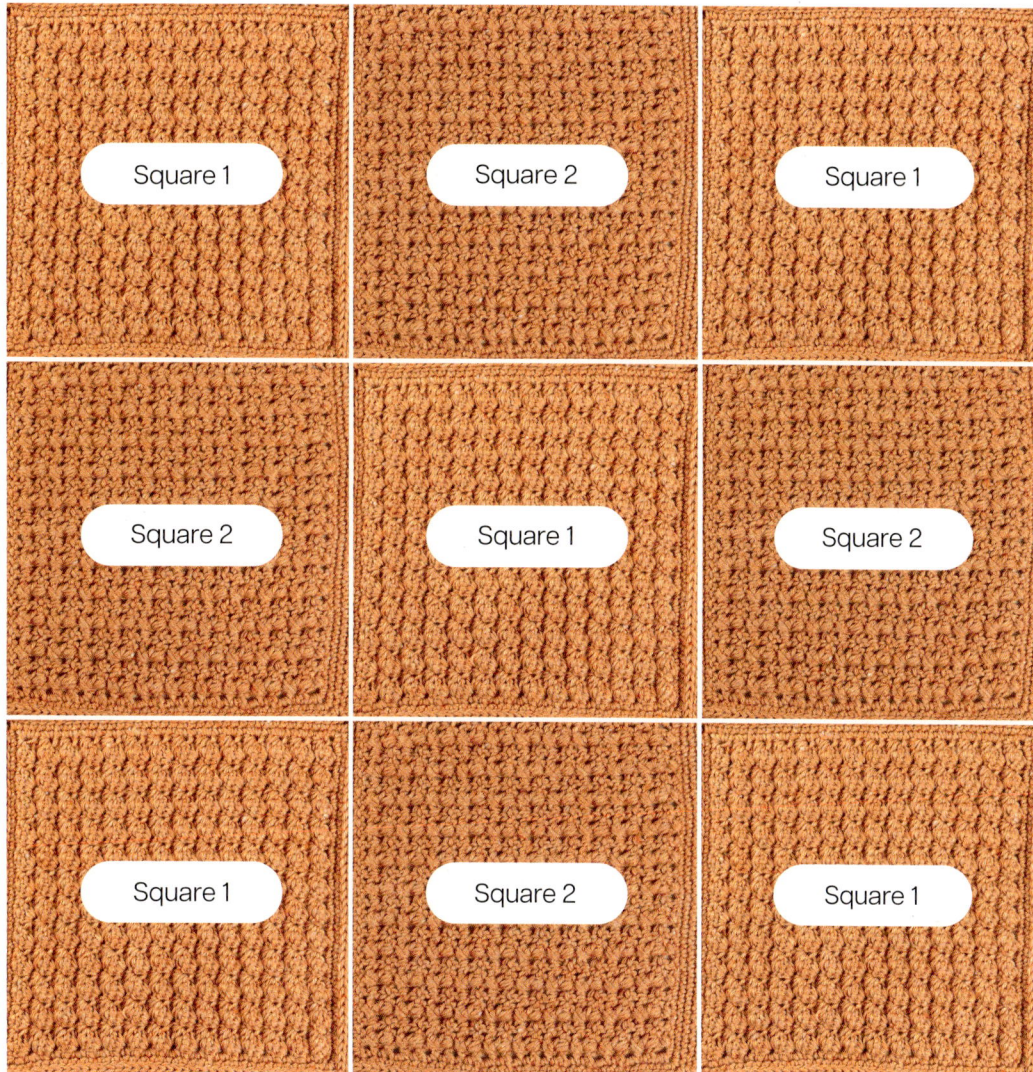

LAYOUT DIAGRAM

Rnd 3: Ch 1, sc in the 1st 2 sc, (sc, ch 2, sc) in corner ch-2 space, *sc in each sc to next corner ch-2 space, (sc, ch 2, sc) in corner ch-2 space; rep from * 2 more times, sc in each remaining sc, join with a sl st to the 1st sc—492 sc, 4 ch-2 spaces.

Rnd 4: Sl st in next st, ch 1, (sc, dc, sc) in same st, sk 1 sc, (sc, ch 2, sc) in corner ch-2 space, [sk 1 sc, (sc, dc, sc) in next sc, *sk 2 sc, (sc, dc, sc) in next sc; rep from * to 1 sc before next corner ch-2 space, sk 1 sc, (sc, ch 2, sc) in corner ch-2 space] 3 times, sk 1 sc, **(sc, dc, sc) in next sc, sk 2 sc; rep from ** to last st, sk last st, join with a sl st to the 1st sc—164 (sc, dc, sc), 4 (sc, ch-2, sc).

Fasten off.

Block.

Weave in ends.

"Love Story" Wedding Shawl

Skill Level

1 2 3 **4**

Designed by Lee Sartori

Imagine arriving at the most perfect wedding. Picture the pretty glowing lights strung up everywhere, the joyful celebration, nostalgic music playing, and the wedding party dressed in elegant gowns and dashing suits. The vibe is pure happiness, and everyone is dressed to the nines!

Transporting you straight into the pages of *Romeo and Juliet*, the "Love Story" Wedding Shawl is the perfect addition to this memorable wedding. Crochet this shawl as an heirloom gift to celebrate the big day or a sweet marriage proposal. With this more advanced-level crochet project, you'll have the chance to try the filet crochet technique! You'll start by crafting a delicate rose that symbolizes love in its purest form. Next, you'll move on to the tender affirmation, "Say Yes"—a nod to the heartwarming narrative of engagements.

Filet crochet is a fun technique that combines double crochet stitches with chain spaces worked in turned rows to create positive and negative space, forming images and text. It's like crocheting a bit of romantic magic into a special keepsake stitch by stitch and row by row. This endearing shawl will be a tangible, heartfelt expression of love made by you! It is a love story, after all.

Measurements

66" x 24" (167.5 x 61 cm)

Yarn

DK weight (#3 Light)

Shown here: Lion Brand 24/7 Cotton DK, 273 yds (249 m), 3½ oz (100 g), 100% cotton: 7 balls 100 Sugarcane

Hook

US size C/2 (2.5 mm) crochet hook. Adjust hook size if necessary to obtain correct gauge.

Notions

Yarn needle

Scissors

Gauge

Gauge is not critical for this project.

1 square measures 11" x 12" (28 x 30.5 cm)

Notes

♥ The Shawl is worked in filet crochet following charts or written instructions. In filet crochet, (dc, ch 2) Open (O) Squares and 3-dc Closed (X) Squares are worked to form patterns. Each row of filet crochet ends with a final double crochet stitch.

♥ Each filet crochet row instruction indicates the number of Open Squares and Closed Squares to work. For example, (O) x 3, (X) x 6, (O) x 1, (X) x 5, (O) x 3, (X) x 2, (O) x 5 means that you will work 3 Open Squares, then 6 Closed Squares, 1 Open Square, 5 Closed Squares, 3 Open Squares, 2 Closed Squares, 5 Open Squares, then end with a dc in last st. The example written using standard crochet terms would read as follows: Ch 5, sk next 2 sts, (dc in next st, ch 2, sk next 2 sts) twice, dc in next 19 sts, ch 2, sk next 2 sts, dc in next 16 sts, ch 2, sk next 2 sts, (dc in next st, ch 2, sk next 2 sts) twice, dc in next 7 sts, ch 2, sk next 2 sts, (dc in next st, ch 2, sk next 2 sts) 4 times, dc in last st.

♥ The filet crochet charts are read from the bottom up. Read RS rows from right to left and WS rows from left to right.

CONTINUED

TAYLOR-MADE FOR YOU

Crochet your "Love Story" Wedding Shawl in a different color to transform it from a wedding piece into an everyday wearable that you can enjoy year-round!

Special Stitches

O (Open Square): Dc in next st, ch 2, sk next 2 sts.

X (Closed Square): Dc in next 3 sts.

beg Open Square: Ch 5, sk next 2 sts.

beg Closed Square: Ch 3, dc in next 2 sts.

"SAY YES" SQUARE (MAKE 6)

Ch 80 and begin in the 8th ch from the hook.

Rows 1 (RS) and 2: (O) x 25.

Row 3 (RS): (O) x 3, (X) x 6, (O) x 1, (X) x 5, (O) x 3, (X) x 2, (O) x 5.

Row 4: (O) x 5, (X) x 2, (O) x 3, (X) x 5, (O) x 1, (X) x 6, (O) x 3.

Row 5: (O) x 3, (X) x 2, (O) x 2, (X) x 2, (O) x 4, (X) x 2, (O) x 3, (X) x 2, (O) x 5.

Row 6: (O) x 5, (X) x 2, (O) x 3, (X) x 2, (O) x 7, (X) x 2, (O) x 4.

Row 7: (O) x 5, (X) x 2, (O) x 3, (X) x 5, (O) x 2, (X) x 4, (O) x 4.

Row 8: (O) x 4, (X) x 4, (O) x 2, (X) x 5, (O) x 2, (X) x 2, (O) x 6.

Row 9: (O) x 3, (X) x 2, (O) x 2, (X) x 2, (O) x 4, (X) x 2, (O) x 1, (X) x 2, (O) x 2, (X) x 2, (O) x 3.

Row 10: (O) x 3, (X) x 2, (O) x 2, (X) x 2, (O) x 1, (X) x 2, (O) x 4, (X) x 2, (O) x 2, (X) x 2, (O) x 3.

Row 11: (O) x 3, (X) x 6, (O) x 1, (X) x 5, (O) x 1, (X) x 2, (O) x 2, (X) x 2, (O) x 3.

Row 12: (O) x 3, (X) x 2, (O) x 2, (X) x 2, (O) x 1, (X) x 5, (O) x 1, (X) x 6, (O) x 3.

Rows 13 and 14: (O) x 25.

Row 15: (O) x 5, (X) x 2, (O) x 3, (X) x 2, (O) x 1, (X) x 2, (O) x 1, (X) x 6, (O) x 3.

Row 16: (O) x 3, (X) x 6, (O) x 1, (X) x 2, (O) x 1, (X) x 2, (O) x 3, (X) x 2, (O) x 5.

Row 17: (O) x 5, (X) x 2, (O) x 3, (X) x 2, (O) x 1, (X) x 2, (O) x 1, (X) x 2, (O) x 2, (X) x 2, (O) x 3.

Row 18: (O) x 6, (X) x 2, (O) x 2, (X) x 5, (O) x 3, (X) x 2, (O) x 5.

Row 19: (O) x 4, (X) x 4, (O) x 2, (X) x 5, (O) x 3, (X) x 2, (O) x 5.

Row 20: (O) x 4, (X) x 2, (O) x 4, (X) x 2, (O) x 1, (X) x 2, (O) x 2, (X) x 4, (O) x 4.

Row 21: (O) x 3, (X) x 2, (O) x 2, (X) x 2, (O) x 1, (X) x 2, (O) x 1, (X) x 2, (O) x 1, (X) x 2, (O) x 2, (X) x 2, (O) x 3.

Row 22: (O) x 3, (X) x 2, (O) x 2, (X) x 2, (O) x 1, (X) x 2, (O) x 1, (X) x 2, (O) x 1, (X) x 2, (O) x 2, (X) x 2, (O) x 3.

Row 23: (O) x 3, (X) x 2, (O) x 2, (X) x 2, (O) x 1, (X) x 5, (O) x 1, (X) x 6, (O) x 3.

Row 24: (O) x 3, (X) x 6, (O) x 2, (X) x 3, (O) x 2, (X) x 2, (O) x 2, (X) x 2, (O) x 3.

Rows 25 and 26: (O) x 25.

Fasten off.

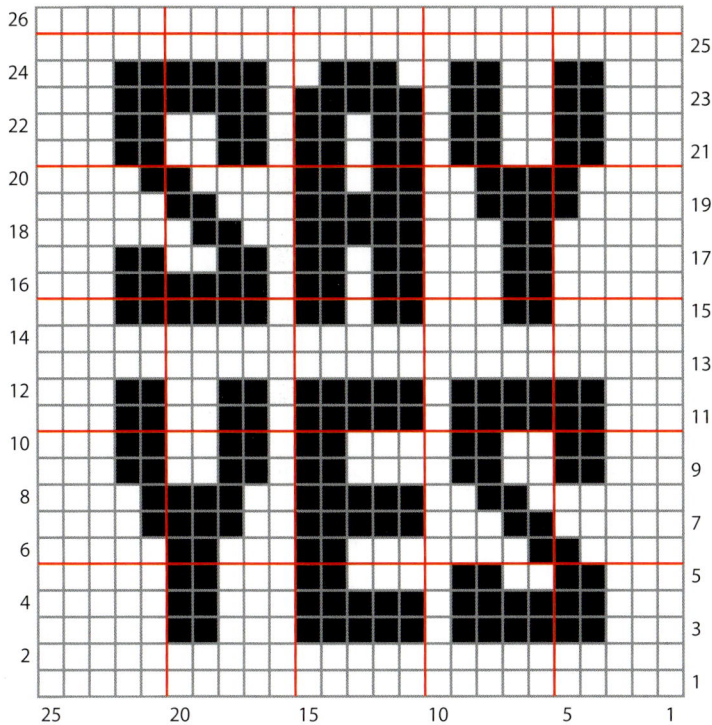

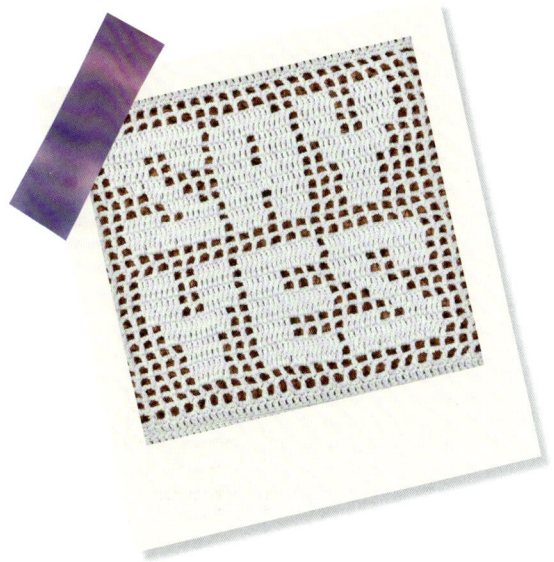

Key

☐ Open Square (Dc in next st, ch 2, sk next 2 sts)

■ Closed Square (Dc in next 3 sts)

☐ beg Open Square (Ch 5, sk next 2 sts)

■ beg Closed Square (Ch 3, dc in next 2 sts)

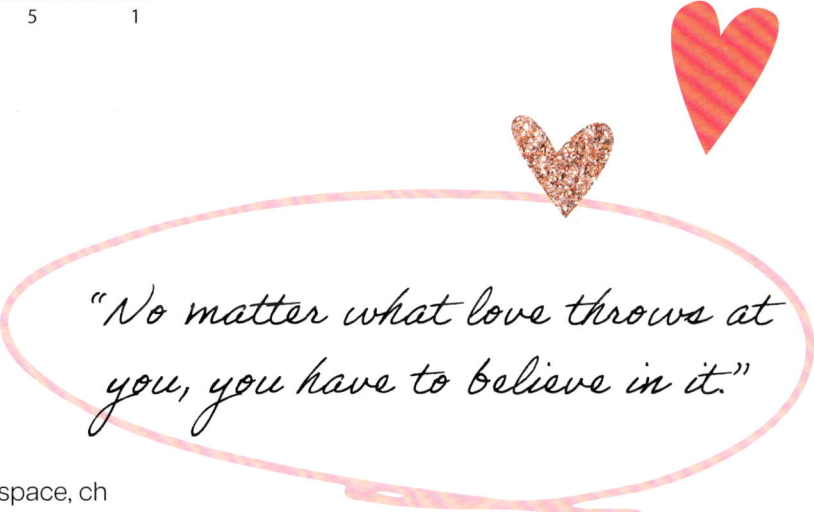

"No matter what love throws at you, you have to believe in it."

—TAYLOR SWIFT

BORDER

Rnd 1: With RS facing, join to top right ch-2 space, ch 1, 2 sc in each ch-2 space across, ch 2 (corner made) and rotate to work across left side, 2 sc in each ch-2 space across, ch 2 (corner made), rotate to work across bottom edge, 2 sc in each ch-2 space across, ch 2 (corner made), rotate to work across right side, 2 sc in each ch-2 space to across to top, ch 2 (final corner made) join to 1st st—204 sc, 4 ch-2 spaces.

Rnd 2: Ch 3 (counts as 1st dc), *dc in each sc across to ch-2 corner, (dc, ch 2, dc) in ch-2 corner; repeat from * around, join—212 dc, 4 ch-2 spaces.

Fasten off, weave in ends.

ROSE SQUARE (MAKE 6)

Ch 80 and begin in the 8th ch from the hook.

Rows 1 (RS) and 2: (O) x 25.

Row 3 (RS): (O) x 11, (X) x 1, (O) x 13.

Row 4: (O) x 13, (X) x 1, (O) x 11.

Row 5: (O) x 11, (X) x 1, (O) x 13.

Row 6: (O) x 13, (X) x 1, (O) x 1, (X) x 2, (O) x 8.

Row 7: (O) x 7, (X) x 5, (O) x 13.

Row 8: (O) x 13, (X) x 1, (O) x 1, (X) x 4, (O) x 6.

Row 9: (O) x 6, (X) x 3, (O) x 2, (X) x 1, (O) x 13.

Row 10: (O) x 13, (X) x 1, (O) x 3, (X) x 2, (O) x 6.

Row 11: (O) x 6, (X) x 1, (O) x 4, (X) x 1, (O) x 13.

Row 12: (O) x 13, (X) x 1, (O) x 11.

Row 13: (O) x 10, (X) x 3, (O) x 12.

Row 14: (O) x 10, (X) x 6, (O) x 9.

Row 15: (O) x 8, (X) x 6, (O) x 1, (X) x 1, (O) x 9.

Row 16: (O) x 8, (X) x 3, (O) x 1, (X) x 6, (O) x 7.

Row 17: (O) x 7, (X) x 5, (O) x 1, (X) x 5, (O) x 7.

Row 18: (O) x 7, (X) x 6, (O) x 1, (X) x 4, (O) x 7.

Row 19: (O) x 7, (X) x 11, (O) x 7.

Row 20: (O) x 7, (X) x 5, (O) x 1, (X) x 1, (O) x 2, (X) x 2, (O) x 7.

Row 21: (O) x 6, (X) x 1, (O) x 3, (X) x 2, (O) x 2, (X) x 5, (O) x 6.

Row 22: (O) x 7, (X) x 3, (O) x 2, (X) x 1, (O) x 2, (X) x 4, (O) x 6.

Row 23: (O) x 7, (X) x 1, (O) x 2, (X) x 2, (O) x 1, (X) x 2, (O) x 10.

Row 24: (O) x 11, (X) x 3, (O) x 1, (X) x 2, (O) x 8.

Rows 25 and 26: (O) x 25.

Fasten off.

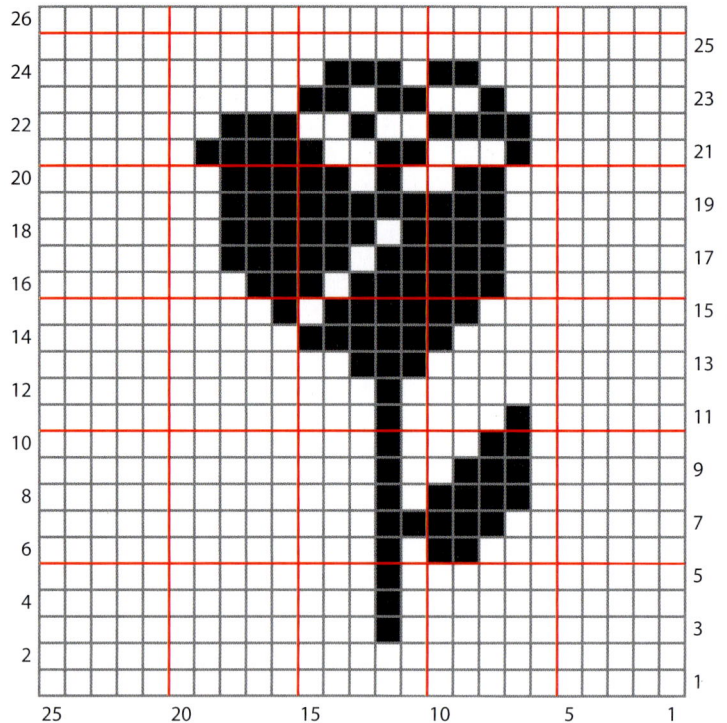

KEY

☐ Open Square (Dc in next st, ch 2, sk next 2 sts)
■ Closed Square (Dc in next 3 sts)
☐ beg Open Square (Ch 5, sk next 2 sts)
■ beg Closed Square (Ch 3, dc in next 2 sts)

BORDER

Rnd 1: With RS facing, join to top right ch-2 space, ch 1, 2 sc in each ch-2 space across, ch 2 (corner made) and rotate to work across left side, 2 sc in each ch-2 space across, ch 2 (corner made), rotate to work across bottom edge, 2 sc in each ch-2 space across, ch 2 (corner made), rotate to work across right side, 2 sc in each ch-2 space across to top, ch 2 (final corner made) join to 1st st—204 sc, 4 ch-2 spaces.

Rnd 2: Ch 3 (counts as 1st dc), *dc in each sc across to ch-2 corner, (dc, ch 2, dc) in ch-2 corner; rep from * around, join—212 dc, 4 ch-2 spaces.

Fasten off, weave in ends.

ASSEMBLY

Join squares using preferred joining method. Sample used sl st on WS to join 2 squares together. Squares should be assembled with 2 rows of 6 squares, alternating the "Say Yes" Square and the Rose Square. Weave in ends and continue to Border.

BORDER

Join to top right corner of assembled shawl.

Rnd 1: Ch 3 (counts as 1st dc), *[dc in each dc across to where 2 squares meet, dc in ch-2 corner space, dc in the fabric of the join between 2 squares, dc in next ch-2 space] across to next ch-2 corner, (dc, ch 2, dc) in ch-2 corner; rep from * around entire shawl.

Fasten off, weave in ends.

FINISHING

Cut approximately 230 pieces of yarn measuring 6" (15 cm) long. Loop each piece through stitches of short edges of shawl and secure to create fringe.

"I am completely fascinated by the differences and comparisons between real life and fairy tales because we're raised as little girls to think that we're a princess and that Prince Charming is going to sweep us off our feet."

—TAYLOR SWIFT

"Enchanted" Graphgan

Skill Level

1 2 **3** 4

Designed by Valérie Prieur-Côté

The "Enchanted" Graphgan seeks to capture that beautiful moment when a furtive glance from across the room sparks the beginning of something new and wonderful. It's about the overwhelming feeling of being alone in your thoughts and insecurities, only to have it all suddenly vanish when you see the right person in front of you. That amazing person who brings you back into the present with a blush and a smile and the playful conversation that marks the first page in a story of love and friendship. They take your hand and lead you into a sparkling night, leaving you wonderstruck and in love.

The "Enchanted" Graphgan features a beautiful silhouette surrounded by butterflies, representing the moment you break away from darkness and step into something wistful and exciting. The blanket is worked in single crochet, so it's a perfect first color work project! Finish it off with a beautiful purple border and you'll be ready to show off something absolutely stunning and awe-inspiring.

Measurements

56" x 78" (142 x 198 cm)

Yarn

Worsted weight (#4 Medium)

Shown here: Lion Brand Basic Stitch Anti-Pilling, 185 yd (169 m), 3½ oz (100 g), 100% acrylic: 12 balls 101 Baby Pink (A), 4 balls 147 Purple (B), 4 balls 122 Hazelnut (C), 3 balls 184 Peachy (D), small amount 400 Red Heather (E)

Hook

US size I/9 (5.5 mm) crochet hook. Adjust hook size if necessary to obtain correct gauge.

Notions

Yarn needle

Scissors

Gauge

14 sts x 16 rows = 4" (10 cm) in sc stitch

Notes

♥ The afghan is worked in rows of single crochet (sc), beginning with a foundation single crochet (Fsc) row, changing yarn color according to the chart.

♥ Each square of the chart represents a single crochet (sc) stitch worked in the indicated color. Begin each row by turning and working a ch 1. Read RS (odd-numbered) rows from right to left and WS (even-numbered) rows from left to right.

♥ The hair color chosen for the pattern is on the darker side of blond; for a lighter blond, use color 121 Almond in the same yarn.

♥ Divide the yarn into smaller balls to make the color work easier.

♥ To change yarn color, work last stitch of previous color to last yarn over. Yarn over with new color and draw through all loops on hook to complete stitch. Drop previous color to WS of afghan. Cut previous color if it won't be used again nearby. If previous color will be needed again nearby, carefully carry it up the WS when next needed.

♥ The graph is upside down to start with a row of only one color.

CONTINUED

Special Stitches

Fsc (foundation single crochet): Ch 2, insert hook in 2nd ch from hook and pull up loop, yo and pull through 1 loop (ch made), yo and pull through 2 loops (sc made), *insert hook in ch of previous st and pull up loop, yo and pull through 1 loop (ch made), yo and pull through 2 loops (sc made); repeat from * for required number of Fsc.

P (Picot): Ch 3, insert hook back into the center of the base stitch, yo, pull through all loops on hook.

GRAPHGAN

Row 1 (RS): With A, Fsc 202.

Rows 2 and 3: With A, ch 1, turn, sc in each st across.

Rows 4–312: Ch 1, turn, sc in each st across AND change yarn color following chart, begin with Row 4 of chart.

Fasten off.

BORDER

With RS facing, join B with sc in top right corner of afghan.

Rnd 1: Sc across the top of blanket, ch 1 at the corner, rotate to work across row ends, sc in each row end, ch1, sc in each ch of the bottom of the afghan, ch 1 at the corner, rotate to work across row ends, sc in each row end, ch 1, sl st into first sc.

Rnd 2: *4 sc, P; rep from * around, sl st into first sc.

Fasten off.

TAYLOR-MADE FOR YOU

For a clean color change, draw the new color through the last yarn over (yo) of the previous stitch! It creates a seamless color transition to make your work pop.

KEY

- ☐ Baby Pink (A)
- ☐ Purple (B)
- ☐ Hazelnut (C)
- ☐ Peachy (D)
- ☐ Red Heather (E)

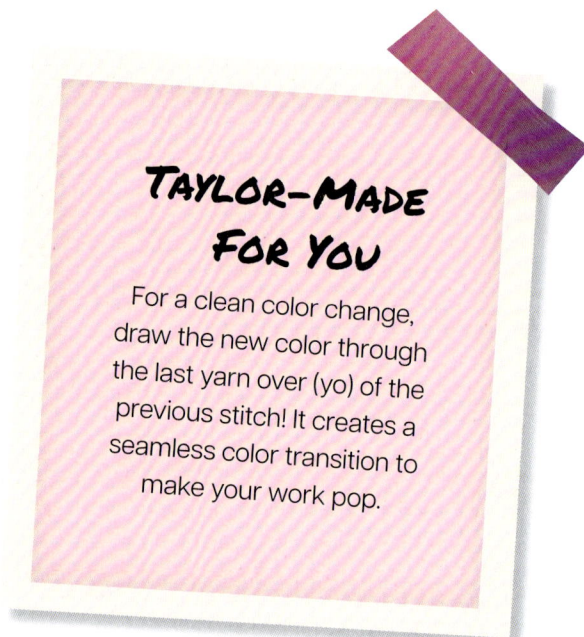

Scan to access complete color charts for this project.

CHAPTER Two

REMINISCE

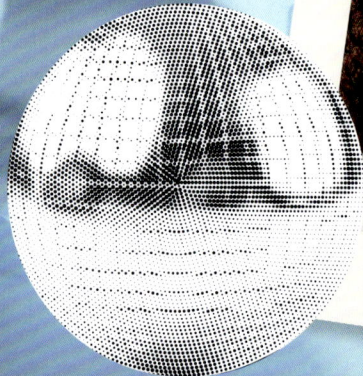

Listening to your favorite songs is a great way to remember the times that have already passed. This chapter takes you on a journey through the past with some beautiful crochet! The "Lavender Haze" Halter Top is a nostalgic piece of iconic crochet. The "Back to December" Hooded Cowl is about fixing mistakes. And the "Marjorie" Granny Square Blanket is about remembering happy times with people we love. All of these crochet projects are perfect for making and sharing with the special people in our lives and taking time to let them know they are appreciated.

"There are so many emotions that you're feeling, you can get stifled by them if you're feeling them all at once. What I try to do is take one moment—one simple, simple feeling—and expand it into three-and-a-half minutes."

—TAYLOR SWIFT

"Lavender Haze" Halter Top

Skill Level 1 2 3 **4**

Designed by Hailey Bailey

Learning how to crochet is such a wonderful experience because it allows you to step back in time to make iconic clothing pieces from decades past. The "Lavender Haze" halter top based on the music video is the perfect example!

"Lavender Haze" by Taylor Swift delves into the complicated feelings that come with the expectations of others, outside scrutiny, and generational pressure. It can be difficult to live the life you want when you are expected to fit into a certain box. It is with love and acceptance that you are able to build the life you envision for yourself. Whether it's the love of a partner or a family member, or even self-love and acceptance, surrounding yourself with an all-encompassing love glow can help release you from outside pressure.

The "Lavender Haze" halter top captures the look of the 1970s, when crochet with bold patterns and colors reigned supreme. Crochet your top in the colors featured in the music video or in colors that are more you. The choice is yours.

Size

XS/S (M, L, 1X, 2X/3X, 4X, 5X)

Choose a size with anywhere between 4–8" (10–20.5 cm) of negative ease, depending on desired fit. The more negative ease, the tighter the fit and the more open back will be visible with the corset tie.

Measurements

Chest circumference: 24½ (31½, 35, 38½, 45½, 49, 56)" [62 (80, 89, 98, 115.5, 124.5, 142) cm]

Length: 15½ (16, 17, 17, 19, 19, 20)" [39.5 (40.5, 43, 43, 48.5, 48.5, 51) cm]

Yarn

Worsted weight (#4 Medium)

Shown here: Lion Brand 24/7 Cotton, 186 yds (170 m), 3½ oz (100 g), 100% cotton: 2 (2, 2, 3, 3, 4, 4) balls 100 White (A), 1 (1, 1, 2, 2, 2, 2) balls 186 Amber (B), 1 (1, 1, 1, 2, 2, 2) balls 158 Goldenrod (C), 1 (1, 1, 1, 2, 2, 2) balls 103 Pink Lemonade (D)

Hook

US size G/6 (4 mm) crochet hook. Adjust hook size if necessary to obtain correct gauge.

Notions

Yarn needle

Stitch markers

Scissors

Gauge

1 chevron = 3½" (9 cm) measured from peak to peak

13 rows of chevron pattern = 5¾" (14.5 cm)

Notes

♥ Turning chains do not count as a stitch throughout pattern.

♥ Halter top is worked bottom up. Piece is divided at underarms and backs and front are worked separately up to neckline.

♥ Yarn color is changed to form stripes. To change yarn color, work last stitch of previous color to last yarn over. Yarn over with new color and draw through all loops on hook to complete stitch. Proceed with new color.

♥ Neckline/back strap is created with a crocheted I-cord, but can be substituted with a cord made with a long row of single crochet if preferred.

CONTINUED

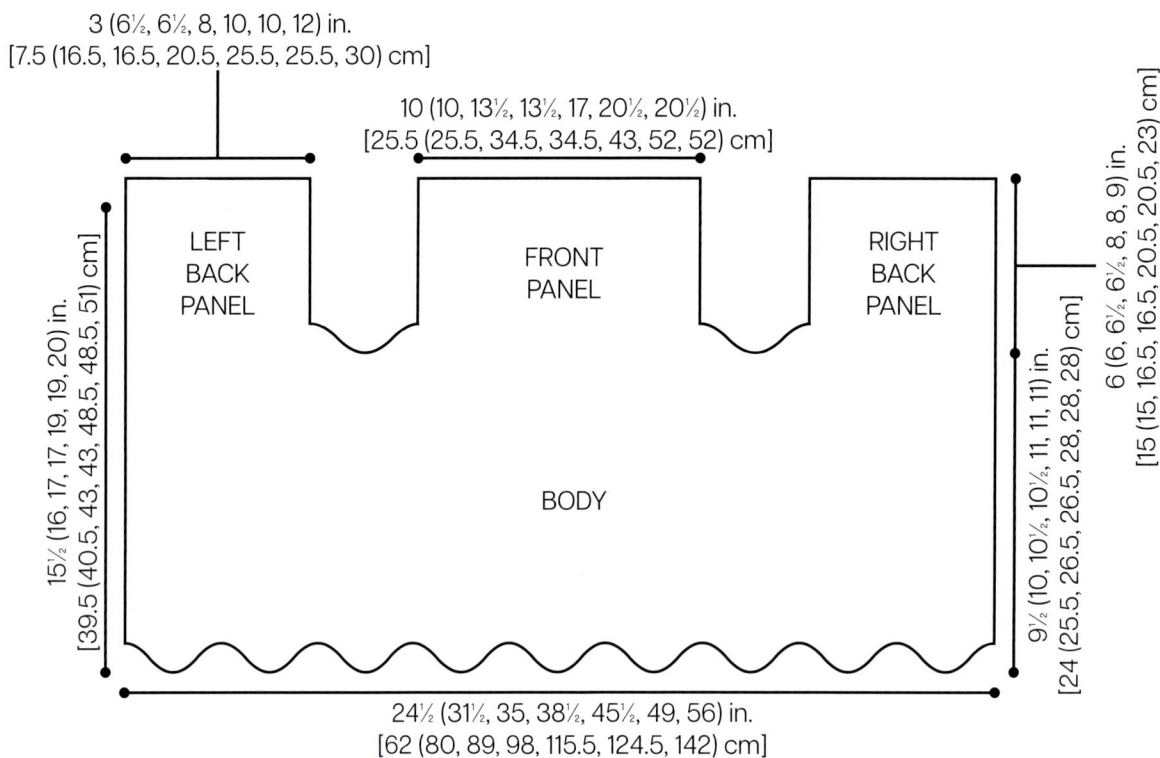

3 (6½, 6½, 8, 10, 10, 12) in.
[7.5 (16.5, 16.5, 20.5, 25.5, 25.5, 30) cm]

10 (10, 13½, 13½, 17, 20½, 20½) in.
[25.5 (25.5, 34.5, 34.5, 43, 52, 52) cm]

6 (6, 6½, 6½, 8, 8, 9) in.
[15 (15, 16.5, 16.5, 20.5, 20.5, 23) cm]

15½ (16, 17, 17, 19, 19, 20) in.
[39.5 (40.5, 43, 43, 48.5, 48.5, 51) cm]

| LEFT BACK PANEL | FRONT PANEL | RIGHT BACK PANEL |

BODY

9½ (10, 10½, 10½, 11, 11, 11) in.
[24 (25.5, 26.5, 26.5, 28, 28, 28) cm]

24½ (31½, 35, 38½, 45½, 49, 56) in.
[62 (80, 89, 98, 115.5, 124.5, 142) cm]

BODY DIAGRAM

BODY

Sizes XS/S (M, L, 2X/3X, 4X) Only

Row 1: With A, ch 98 (126, 140, 182, 196), 2 dc in 3rd ch from hook, dc 3, [dc2tog] twice, *dc 4, [2 dc in next st] twice, dc 4, [dc2tog] twice, rep from * to last 4 ch, dc 3, 2 dc in last ch, turn—96 (124, 138, 180, 194) dc (7 (9, 10, 13, 14) chevrons).

Row 2: Ch 2 (does not count as a st here or throughout), 2 dc, dc 3, [dc2tog] twice, *dc 4, [2 dc in next st] twice, dc 4, [dc2tog] twice, rep from * to last 4 sts, dc 3, 2 dc in last st, turn.

Change to B and proceed to Row 3.

TAYLOR-MADE FOR YOU

Wear the "Lavender Haze" halter top with a pair of brown corduroy pants to complete the look!

Sizes 1X (5X) Only

Row 1: With A, ch 154 (224), dc2tog in 3rd and 4th ch from hook, dc 3, [2 dc in next st] twice, *dc 4, [dc2tog] twice, dc 4, [2 dc in next st] twice, rep from * to last 5 ch, dc 3, dc2tog, turn—152 (222) dc (11 (14) chevrons).

Row 2: Ch 2 (does not count as a st here or throughout), dc2tog, dc 3, [2 dc in next st] twice, *dc 4, [dc2tog] twice, dc 4, [2 dc in next st] twice, rep from * to last 5 sts, dc 3, dc2tog, turn.

Change to B and proceed to Row 3.

All Sizes

Rows 3–22 (23, 24, 24, 25, 25, 25): Rep Row 2 for 20 (21, 22, 22, 23, 23, 23) more rows, following Stripe Sequence as follows:

Work 1 row with B, 1 row with D, 1 row with B, 1 row with C, 4 (5, 6, 6, 7, 7, 7) rows with A, 1 row with C, 1 row with B, 1 row with A, 1 row with B, 1 row with D, 1 row with B, 1 row with D, 1 row with B, 1 row with D, 1 row with B, 1 row with C, 1 row with A. Do not change yarn color at the end of last row.

With last row worked facing, place a marker on last row to indicate RS.

Place 3 more markers accordingly:

XS/S: 28th, 69th, and 84th sts.

M: 42nd, 83rd, and 98th sts.

L: 42nd, 97th, and 112th sts.

1X: 49th, 104th, and 119th sts.

2X/3X: 56th, 125th, and 140th sts.

4X: 56th, 139th, and 154th sts.

5X: 63rd, 146th, and 161st sts.

First marker indicates where the front panel will begin, 2nd marker indicates where front panel will end, and 3rd marker indicates where the left back panel will begin.

RIGHT BACK PANEL
Size XS/S Only

Row 1: With A, ch 2, 2 dc, dc 3, [dc2tog] twice, dc 5; leave rem sts unworked, turn—12 sts (1 chevron).

Row 2: Ch 2, 2 dc, dc 3, [dc2tog] twice, dc 3, 2 dc, turn.

Rows 3–12: Rep Row 2 for 10 more rows, following Stripe Sequence as follows: Work 1 row with C, 1 row with B, 1 row with D, 1 row with A, 1 row with B, 1 row with C, 1 row with D, 1 row with B, 2 rows with A.

Row 13: With A, ch 1, sc, hdc 3, dc 4, hdc 3, sc 1, turn.

Fasten off and proceed to Front Panel.

Sizes M (L) Only

Row 1: With A, ch 2, 2 dc, dc 3, [dc2tog] twice, dc 4, [2 dc in next st] twice, dc 4, [dc2tog] twice, dc 5; leave rem sts unworked, turn—26 sts (2 chevrons).

Row 2: Ch 2, 2 dc, dc 3, [dc2tog] twice, dc 4, [2 dc in next st] twice, dc 4, [dc2tog] twice, dc 3, 2 dc, turn.

Rows 3–12 (14): Rep Row 2 for 10 (12) more rows, following Stripe Sequence as follows: Work 0 (2) rows with A, 1 row with C, 1 row with B, 1 row with D, 1 row with A, 1 row with B, 1 row with C, 1 row with D, 1 row with B, 2 rows with A.

Row 13 (15): With A, ch 1, sc, hdc 3, dc 4, hdc 3, sc 4, hdc 3, dc 4, hdc 3, sc, turn.

Fasten off and proceed to Front Panel.

3 (3, 3½, 3½, 4, 4½, 5) in.
[7.5 (7.5, 9, 9, 10, 11.5, 12.5) cm]

STRAP

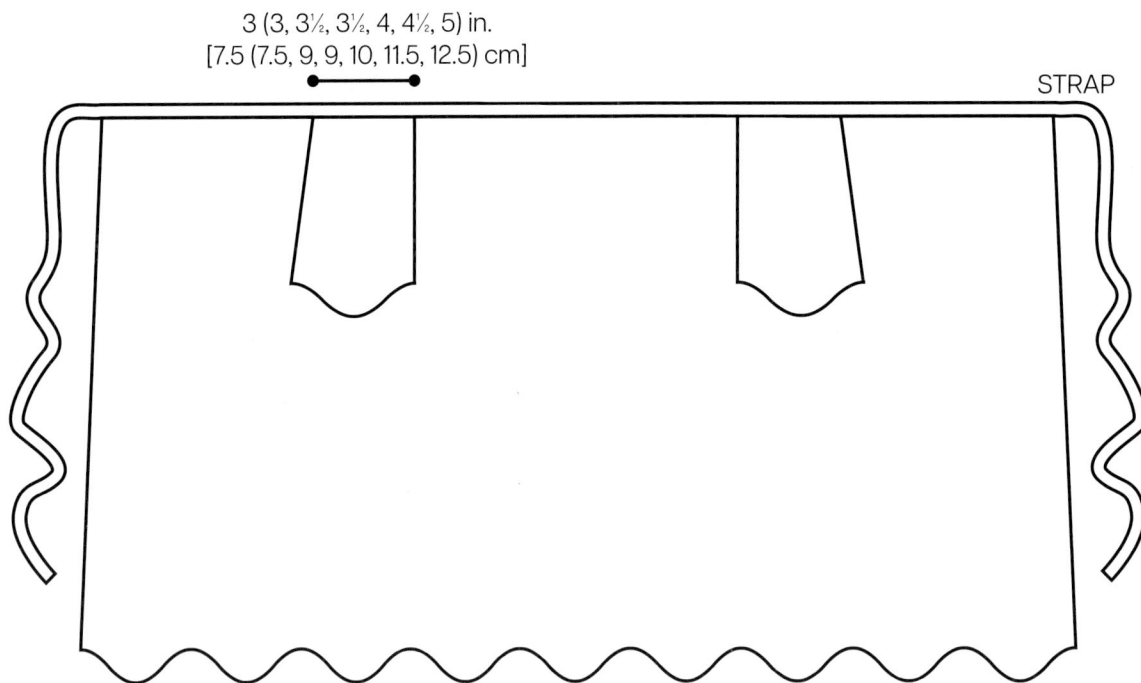

STRAP ATTACHMENT DIAGRAM

Size 1X Only

Row 1: With A, ch 2, dc2tog, dc 3, [2 dc in next st] twice, dc 4, [dc2tog] twice, dc 4, [2 dc in next st] twice, dc 4, [dc2tog] twice, dc 5; leave rem sts unworked, turn—33 sts (2.5 chevrons).

Row 2: Ch 2, 2 dc, dc 3, [dc2tog] twice, dc 4, [2 dc in next st] twice, dc 4, [dc2tog] twice, dc 4, [2 dc in next st] twice, dc 3, dc2tog, turn.

Row 3: Ch 2, dc2tog, dc 3, [2 dc in next st] twice, dc 4, [dc2tog] twice, dc 4, [2 dc in next st] twice, dc 4, [dc2tog] twice, dc 3, 2 dc, turn.

Rows 4–14: Rep Rows 2 and 3 for 11 more rows, ending with a Row 2, following Stripe Sequence as follows: Work 1 row with A, 1 row with C, 1 row with B, 1 row with D, 1 row with A, 1 row with B, 1 row with C, 1 row with D, 1 row with B, 2 rows with A.

Row 15: With A, ch 2, dc, [hdc 3, sc 4, hdc 3, dc 4] twice, hdc 3, sc, turn.

Fasten off and proceed to Front Panel.

Sizes 2X/3X (4X) Only

Row 1: With A, ch 2, 2 dc, dc 3, [dc2tog] twice, *dc 4, [2 dc in next st] twice, dc 4, [dc2tog] twice; rep from * once more, dc 5; leave rem sts unworked, turn—40 sts (3 chevrons).

Row 2: Ch 2, 2 dc, dc 3, [dc2tog] twice, * dc 4, [2 dc in next st] twice, dc 4, [dc2tog] twice; rep from * once more, dc 3, 2 dc, turn.

Rows 3–17: Rep Row 2 for 15 more rows, following Stripe Sequence as follows: Work 5 rows with A, 1 row with C, 1 row with B, 1 row with D, 1 row with A, 1 row with B, 1 row with C, 1 row with D, 1 row with B, 2 rows with A.

Row 18: With A, ch 1, sc, [hdc 3, dc 4, hdc 3, sc 4] twice, hdc 3, dc 4, hdc 3, sc, turn.

Fasten off and proceed to Front Panel.

Size 5X Only

Row 1: With A, ch 2, dc2tog, dc 3, *[2 dc in next st] twice, dc 4, [dc2tog] twice, dc 4; rep from * once more, [2 dc in next st] twice, dc 4, [dc2tog] twice, dc 5; leave rem sts unworked, turn—47 sts (3.5 chevrons).

Row 2: Ch 2, 2 dc, dc 3, *[dc2tog] twice, dc 4, [2 dc in next st] twice, dc 4; rep from * once more, [dc2tog] twice, dc 4, [2 dc in next st] twice, dc 3, dc2tog, turn—47 sts.

Row 3: Ch 2, dc2tog, dc 3, *[2 dc in next st] twice, dc 4, [dc2tog] twice, dc 4; rep from * once more, [2 dc in next st] twice, dc 4, [dc2tog] twice, dc 3, 2 dc, turn.

Rows 4–19: Rep Rows 2 and 3 for 16 more rows, ending with a Row 3, following Stripe Sequence as follows: Work 6 rows with A, 1 row with C, 1 row with B, 1 row with D, 1 row with A, 1 row with B, 1 row with C, 1 row with D, 1 row with B, 2 rows with A.

Row 20: With A, ch 2, dc, [hdc 3, sc 4, hdc 3, dc 4] 3 times, hdc 3, sc, turn.

Fasten off and proceed to Front Panel.

FRONT PANEL

All Sizes

With RS facing, attach A at first marked st, remove marker.

Row 1: Ch 2, dc 5, [dc2tog] twice, *dc 4, [2 dc in next st] twice, dc 4, [dc2tog] twice, rep from * to 4 sts before next marker, dc 5, remove marker, turn—40 (40, 54, 54, 68, 82, 82) sts.

Row 2: Ch 2, 2 dc, dc 3, [dc2tog] twice, *dc 4, [2 dc in next st] twice, dc 4, [dc2tog] twice, rep from * to last 4 sts, dc 3, 2 dc, turn.

Rows 3–12 (12, 14, 14, 17, 17, 19): Rep Row 2 for 10 (10, 12, 12, 15, 15, 17) more rows, following Stripe Sequence as follows: Work 0 (0, 2, 2, 5, 5, 7) rows with A, 1 row with C, 1 row with B, 1 row with D, 1 row with A, 1 row with B, 1 row with C, 1 row with D, 1 row with B, 2 rows with A.

Row 13 (13, 15, 15, 18, 18, 20): Ch 1, sc, hdc 3, dc 4, *hdc 3, sc 4, hdc 3, dc 4, rep from * to last 4 sts, hdc 3, sc, turn.

Fasten off.

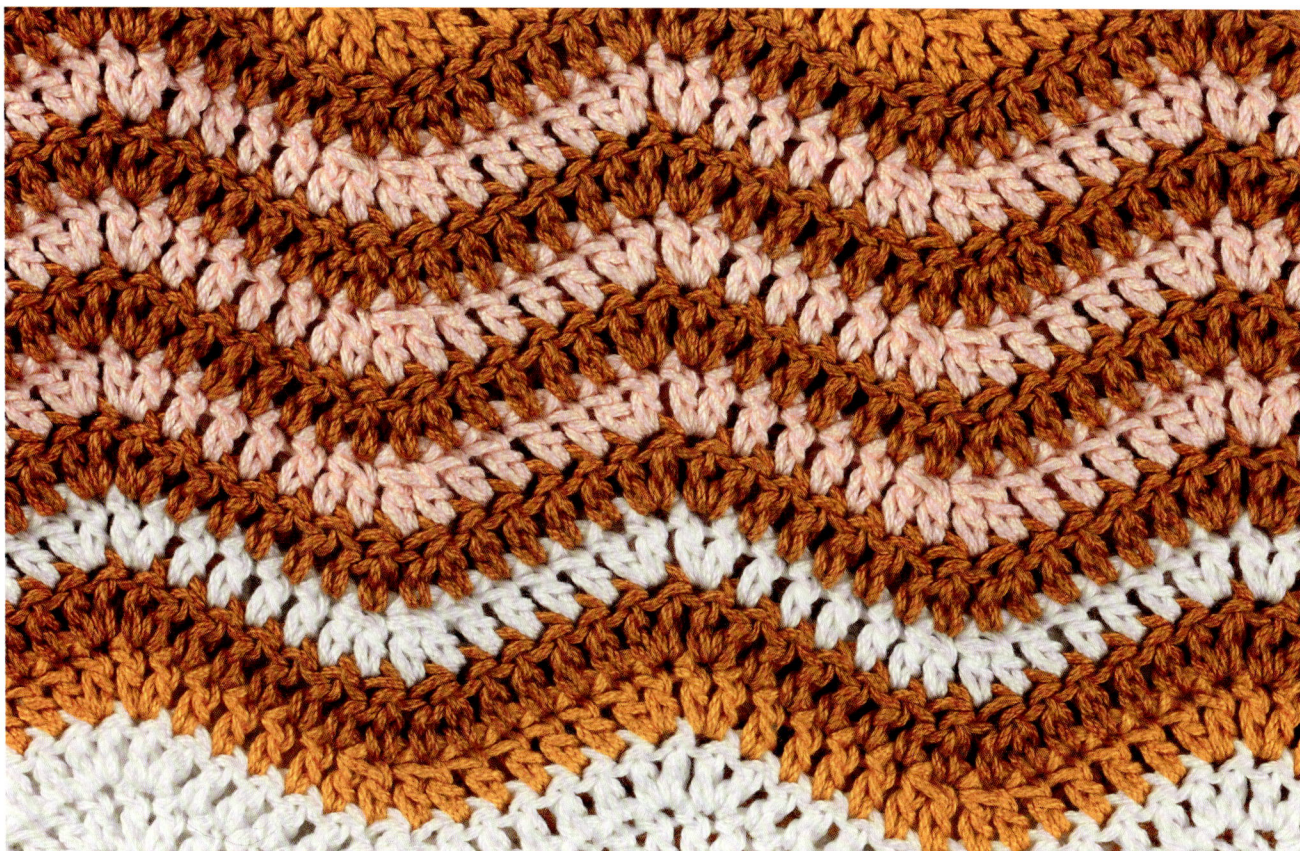

"And it turns out that it's a common phrase used in the '50s where they would just describe being in love, like, you were in the lavender haze, and that meant that you were in that all-encompassing love glow, and I thought that was really beautiful."

—TAYLOR SWIFT

LEFT BACK PANEL

With RS facing, attach A at last remaining marked st, remove marker.

Size XS/S Only

Row 1: Ch 2, dc 5, [dc2tog] twice, dc 3, 2 dc, turn—12 sts.

Rows 2–13: Rep Rows 2-13 of Right Back Panel.

Fasten off and proceed to Strap.

Sizes M (L) Only

Row 1: Ch 2, dc 5, [dc2tog] twice, dc 4, [2 dc in next st] twice, dc 4, [dc2tog] twice, dc 3, 2 dc, turn—26 sts.

Rows 2–13 (15): Rep Rows 2–13 (15) of Right Back Panel.

Fasten off and proceed to Strap.

Size 1X Only

Row 1: Ch 2, dc 5, [dc2tog] twice, dc 4, [2 dc in next st] twice, dc 4, [dc2tog] twice, dc 4, [2 dc in next st] twice, dc 3, dc2tog, turn—33 sts.

Row 2: Ch 2, dc2tog, dc 3, [2 dc in next st] twice, dc 4, [dc2tog] twice, dc 4, [2 dc in next st] twice, dc 4, [dc2tog] twice, dc 3, 2 dc, turn.

Row 3: Ch 2, 2 dc, dc 3, [dc2tog] twice, dc 4, [2 dc in next st] twice, dc 4, [dc2tog] twice, dc 4, [2 dc in next st] twice, dc 3, dc2tog, turn.

Rows 4–14: Rep Row 2-3 for 11 more rows, ending with a Row 2, following Stripe Sequence as follows: Work 1 row with A, 1 row with C, 1 row with B, 1 row with D, 1 row with A, 1 row with B, 1 row with C, 1 row with D, 1 row with B, 2 rows with A.

Row 15: With A, ch 1, sc, [hdc 3, dc 4, hdc 3, sc 4] twice, hdc 3, dc, turn.

Fasten off and proceed to Strap.

Sizes 2X/3X (4X) Only

Row 1: Ch 2, dc 5, [dc2tog] twice, dc 4, [2 dc in next st] twice, dc 4, [dc2tog] twice, dc 4, [2 dc in next st] twice, dc 4, [dc2tog] twice, dc 3, 2 dc, turn—40 sts.

Rows 2–18: Rep Rows 2-18 of Right Back Panel.

Fasten off and proceed to Strap.

Size 5X Only

Row 1: Ch 2, dc 5, *[dc2tog] twice, dc 4, [2 dc in next st] twice, dc 4; rep from * once more, [dc2tog] twice, dc 4, [2 dc in next st] twice, dc 3, dc2tog, turn—47 sts.

Row 2: Ch 2, dc2tog, dc 3, *[2 dc in next st] twice, dc 4, [dc2tog] twice, dc 4; rep from * once more, [2 dc in next st] twice, dc 4, [dc2tog] twice, dc 3, 2 dc, turn.

Row 3: Ch 2, 2 dc, dc 3, *[dc2tog] twice, dc 4, [2 dc in next st] twice, dc 4; rep from * once more, [dc2tog] twice, dc 4, [2 dc in next st] twice, dc 3, dc2tog, turn.

Rows 4–19: Rep Rows 2 and 3 for 16 more rows, ending with a Row 3, following Stripe Sequence as follows: Work 6 rows with A, 1 row with C, 1 row with B, 1 row with D, 1 row with A, 1 row with B, 1 row with C, 1 row with D, 1 row with B, 2 rows with A.

Row 20: With A, ch 1, sc, [hdc 3, dc 4, hdc 3, sc 4] 3 times, hdc 3, dc, turn.

Fasten off and proceed to Strap.

STRAP

With A, create a crocheted I-cord measuring 84 (92, 98, 108, 124, 132, 148)" [213.5 (233.5, 249, 274.5, 315, 335.5, 376) cm].

Note: Length may vary according to amount of negative ease, number of desired strap crosses in back, and desired loose length of cord for tie at hem. Test the length as you go by pinning the cord to your garment and trying it on.

If desired, I-cord can be substituted by a long chain of foundation sc sts.

FINISHING

Weave in all ends.

To attach I-cord strap to garment, place a marker at approximate center point of the I-cord. Attach this point to the center of the front panel using the marker. Using sewing stitch of choice, sew I-cord along top edge of front panel. Allow 3 (3, 3½, 3½, 4, 4½, 5)" [7½ (7½, 9, 9, 10, 11½, 12½) cm] of I-cord space for each shoulder strap, then continue to sew I-cord along top edge of each back panel. With back panels facing, weave both ends of cord, crossing over one another down the back (as with a shoelace), inserting the cord between the first and second sts of a row, alternating about every 6–8 rows or as desired. Loose ends of I-cord will end up at the bottom hem to be tied when wearing.

"Back to December" Hooded Cowl

Skill Level 1 2 **3** 4

Designed by Ashlee Elle

I don't think many of us can say that we have zero regrets. It could be something that we said in anger or maybe something that we did to cause hurt, but either way, the recollection haunts us over and over again. Imagine a world where every regret could be mended and we could sincerely apologize to make things right. I'm sure anyone would gladly take that opportunity.

In "Back to December," Taylor Swift does just that. The song is a melancholy imagining of a conversation that fixes a mistake. It's about making time for someone you love and catching up. It's creating an opportunity to express regret and ask for forgiveness. A chance to remember the good times and take ownership of our actions. It's a beautiful love letter filled with longing for the past and the need to heal.

The "Back to December" Hooded Cowl is the perfect crochet piece to bring warmth in a chilly winter. It features beautiful chunky crochet stitches and a white fur lining reminiscent of falling snow swirling around your face. Crochet one in your favorite color and be ready for warmth and comfort when the cold comes your way this December.

Measurements

Collar circumference: 24" (61 cm)

Height: 13" (33 cm)

Yarn

Chunky weight (#5 Bulky)

Shown here: Lion Brand Basic Stitch Anti-Pilling Thick & Quick, 87 yds (79.5 m), 3½ oz (100 g), 65% recycled polyester, 35% Amicor acrylic: 3 balls 147 Lilac (A)

Super Bulky (#6 Super Bulky)

Shown here: Lion Brand Go For Faux, 65 yds (59 m), 3½ oz (100 g), 100% polyester: 1 ball 098 Baked Alaska (B)

Hooks

US size K/10.5 (6.5 mm) crochet hook, US size N-13 (9 mm) crochet hook. Adjust hook size if necessary to obtain correct gauge.

Notions

Stitch markers

Scissors

Yarn needle

Gauge

Gauge is not critical for this project.

8 hdc x 6 rows = 4" (10 cm)

Notes

♥ The hood is worked from the lower edge upwards.

♥ The collar is worked in rounds, except for the first row. The hood is then worked back and forth in rows over half of the collar stitches and edges of last row, which are seamed to form top of hood.

♥ Faux fur trim is worked around front edge of hood and a drawstring is crocheted and thread through ch-spaces of Rnd 3 of collar.

CONTINUED

TAYLOR-MADE FOR YOU

Use leftover white fur to add pom-poms to the end of the cowl ties for an even softer touch!

HOOD

Row 1: Ch 2, [hdc in next st, 2 hdc in next st] 12 times; leave remaining sts unworked, turn—36 hdc.

Rows 2–14: Ch 2, hdc 36, turn.

Row 15: Ch 1, sc 36, turn—36 sc.

Fasten off.

Fold Row 15 in half, matching 18 sc along halves. Sew or single crochet the edges of Row 15 together to form top of hood. To sew the edges together, cut a piece of yarn measuring approximately 17" (43 cm) long and thread it onto the yarn needle. With WS facing, sew edges together. To crochet the edges together, working through both thicknesses, join A with sc in first st, sc across. Fasten off.

FRONT EDGING

With RS facing and smaller hook, join A in front edge of hood.

Rnd 1: Ch 1, work evenly 60 sc around edge of hood, join.

Rnd 2: Ch 1, *sk 1 st, sc in next 3 sts, ch 1; rep from * around, join—69 sts.

FAUX FUR TRIM

Change to larger hook and B.

Rnd 1: Ch 2, hdc in each ch-1 space around, skipping sc sts; join.

Fasten off.

Weave in all ends.

DRAWSTRING

With smaller hook and A, ch 74 or until drawstring measures approximately 29" (73.5 cm) long. Fasten off.

Use your fingers to weave drawstring in and out of the ch-1 spaces of Rnd 3 (drawstring rnd) of the collar.

COLLAR

With larger hook and A, ch 48; sl st in first ch to form a circle, taking care not to twist chain.

Rnd 1: Ch 2 (does not count as a st), hdc in same ch as joining sl st and in each ch around; join with sl st in first hdc—48 hdc.

Rnd 2: Ch 2 (does not count as a st), hdc 48; join with sl st in first hdc.

Rnd 3 (drawstring casing): Ch 3 (counts as hdc, ch 1), *sk 1 st, hdc in next 3 sts, ch 1; rep from* around, join with sl st in 2nd ch of beg ch-3—24 hdc and 24 ch-1 spaces.

Rnds 4–5: Ch 2, hdc in each hdc and ch-1 space around, join—48 hdc.

"When you are missing someone, time seems to move slower, and when I'm falling in love with someone, time seems to be moving faster."

—TAYLOR SWIFT

Evermore *Taylor Doll*

Designed by Lee Sartori

Hey, hey, hey crocheters! Are you ready to make a tiny version of Taylor? Crocheting amigurumi toys is not just a craft; it can be an adventure of fun and creativity. Amigurumi is the Japanese term for "worked in the round" and if you're a crocheter you have probably tried your hand at this fun technique of making cute stuffies and animals. Now, picture creating a tiny Taylor doll that's not only adorable but also uniquely yours. If this is your first time crocheting an amigurumi, this is a great place to start! There are some pretty fantastic tips and tricks to learn.

This Taylor doll amigurumi project promises loads of excitement. Starting from the bottom up, the journey begins with the creation of the doll's tiny feet, worked upwards towards her no-sew arms, and finishing off with her blond hair. This doll captures the beautiful coat that Taylor wears on the *Evermore* album cover, a retro full-length number. The album is all about reflection and the cozy vibes that come with the fall and winter seasons. Be sure to grab a cup of hot chocolate, snuggle up with your warm blanket, and stitch the day away.

Measurements

14" (35.6 cm) tall x 4" (10.2 cm) wide

Yarn

Worsted weight (#4 Medium)

Shown here: Lion Brand Basic Stitch Anti-Pilling, 185 yds (169 m), 3½ oz (100 g), 100% acrylic: 1 skein each 121 Almond (A), 130 Grass (B), 126 Mahogany (C), 153 Black (D), 158 Mustard (E), 128 Ebony (F), 133 Pumpkin (G)

Hook

US size D/3 (3.25 mm) crochet hook. Adjust hook size if necessary to obtain correct gauge.

Notions

Fiberfill

12 mm black or blue safety eyes

Black embroidery thread

White embroidery thread

Yarn needle

Stitch markers

Scissors

3 small black or brown buttons

Gauge

Gauge is not critical for this project.

24 sc x 26 rows = 4" (10 cm)

Notes

♥ The doll is worked from the bottom up, with arms made separately and added in as the body progresses.

♥ Jacket color work: Change colors by drawing up the new color through the last yo of the working stitch. Stitch over the dropped yarn for 1 stitch after the color change and then float the dropped yarn behind the stitches until the next color change picks up.

Special Stitches

hdc2tog (half double crochet 2 together): Yo and insert hook in indicated st, yo and draw up a loop, yo and insert hook into next st, yo draw up a loop, yo and draw through all loops on hook.

hdc3tog (half double crochet 3 together): Yo and insert hook in indicated st, yarn over and draw up a loop, [yo and insert hook into next st, yo and draw up a loop] twice, yo and draw through all loops on hook.

inv-dec (invisible single crochet decrease): Insert hook in front loop only of each of next 2 sts, yarn over and draw through both sts, yarn over and draw through 2 loops on hook—1 st decreased.

CONTINUED

TAYLOR-MADE FOR YOU

Taylor has so many wonderful outfits from her tours and music videos! You can use the amigurumi instructions as a base and add your own personal touches to bring new outfits to life!

ARMS (MAKE 2)

With A.

Rnd 1: Ch 5, beg in 2nd ch from hook, sc 3, 3 sc in next ch, rotate to work on the underside of ch, sc 3, 3 sc in last ch—12 sc.

Place marker in last sc made to indicate end of rnd. Move marker up as each rnd is completed.

Rnd 2: Sc 4, 2 sc in next st, sc 5, 2 sc in next st, sc in last st—14 sc.

Rnd 3: Sc around.

Rnd 4: Sc 6, ch 3, 3 sc in 2nd ch from hook (thumb made), sc in next ch, sc 8—18 sc.

Rnd 5: Sc 6, sk 4 sc of thumb, sc 8—14 sc.

Rnd 6: [Sc 5, inv-dec] twice—12 sc.

Stuff hand; continue stuffing arm as work progresses.

Rnd 7: [Sc 4, inv-dec] twice—10 sc.

Change to B.

Rnds 8–22: Sc around.

Fasten off, set aside to join to Body at indicated rnd.

SHOES (MAKE 2)

With C.

Rnd 1: Ch 9, sc in 2nd ch from hook, sc 6, 3 sc in next ch, rotate to work on the underside of ch, sc 7, 3 sc in last ch—20 sc.

Place marker in last sc made to indicate end of rnd. Move marker up as each rnd is completed.

Rnd 2: Sc 7, 2 sc in each of next 3 sts, sc 8, 3 sc in next st, sc in last st—25 sc.

Rnd 3: Sc 7, [2 sc, sc in next] x 3, sc 9, 3 sc in next, sc in last 2 sts—30 sc.

Fasten off 1st piece. Repeat Rnd 1–3 for 2nd piece, but do not fasten off.

Rnd 4: With 2 pieces atop one another and working through both thicknesses, sc around—30 sc.

Rnd 5: Sc 7, [sc, inv-dec] x 3, sc 14—27 sc.

Rnd 6: Sc 7, inv-dec, hdc2tog x 2, inv-dec, sc 12—23 sts.

Rnd 7: Sc, inv-dec x 3, hdc3tog x 2, inv-dec x 3, sc 2, inv-dec—12 sts.

Fasten off, stuff the shoe firmly. Continue to Legs.

LEGS (MAKE 2)

Join D to back of heel.

Rnds 1–5: Ch 1, sc around, join with a sl st to first st—12 sc.

Rnd 6: Ch 1, sc 11, 2 sc in last st, join—13 sc.

Rnd 7: Ch 1, sc 12, 2 sc in last st, join—14 sc.

Rnd 8: Ch 1, sc 13, 2 sc in last st, join—15 sc.

Rnds 9–10: Ch 1, sc around, join—15 sc.

Rnd 11: Sc around, do not join.

Rnd 12: Sc 3, [sc, 2 sc in next st] x 4, sc 4—19 sc.

Rnd 13: Sc 5, inv-dec, [2 sc, sc in next] x 3, 2 sc in next st, inv-dec, sc 3—21 sc.

Rnd 14: Sc 6, inv-dec x 6, sc 3—15 sc.

Rnd 15: [Sc 4, 2 sc in next st] around—18 sc.

Rnd 16: [Sc 5, 2 sc in next st] around—21 sc.

Rnd 17: [Sc 6, 2 sc in next st] around—24 sc.

Rnds 18–25: Sc around.

Fasten off. Stuff legs. Continue to Body.

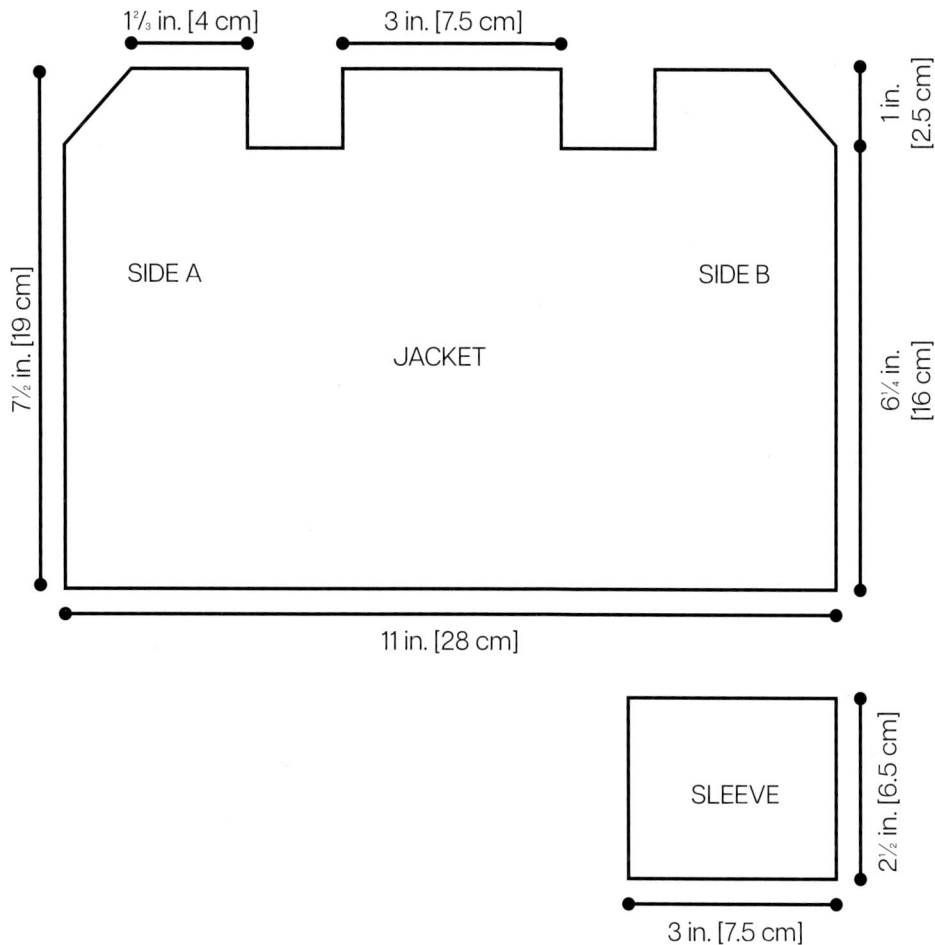

Diagram

1⅔ in. [4 cm]   3 in. [7.5 cm]

1 in. [2.5 cm]

7½ in. [19 cm]

SIDE A   JACKET   SIDE B

6¼ in. [16 cm]

11 in. [28 cm]

SLEEVE

2½ in. [6.5 cm]

3 in. [7.5 cm]

BODY

With D.

With back of Legs facing, mark st in middle of each inner thigh where legs will join.

Rnd 1: With back of Legs facing and beginning in marked st, sc 24 around 1st leg, ch 3, sc in marked st of 2nd leg, sc around—48 sc, ch-3.

Place marker in last sc made to indicate end of rnd. Move marker up as each rnd is completed.

Rnd 2: Sc in each of next 3 ch, sc 24, sc in underside of next 3 ch, sc 24—54 sc.

Rnd 3: 2 sc in next st, 3 sc in next st, 2 sc in next 2 sts, sc around to last st, 2 sc in last st—60 sc.

Rnds 4–12: Sc around.

Rnd 13: Sc 4, sc3tog, sc 4, sc3tog, sc around to last 3 sts, sc3tog—54 sc.

Rnds 14–16: Sc around.

Change to A.

Rnds 17–23: Sc around.

Incorporate arms into next rnd.

Rnd 24: Sc 19, sc 10 around arm ensuring that thumb is facing body, sc 27, sc 10 around arm ensuring that thumb is facing body, sc 8—74 sc.

Rnd 25: Sc 23, inv-dec, sc 35, inv-dec, sc 12—72 sc.

"I wanted Evermore to represent fall & winter while Folklore represents spring & summer. I've always wanted to do a 2part anthology that's a collective body of work & it just kind of happened naturally."

—TAYLOR SWIFT

Rnd 26: [Sc 5, inv-dec, sc 5] around—66 sc.

Rnd 27: [Sc 9, inv-dec] around—60 sc.

Stuff arms and body, continue stuffing as work progresses.

Rnd 28: [Sc 4, inv-dec, sc 4] around—54 sc.

Rnd 29: [Sc 7, inv-dec] around—48 sc.

Rnd 30: [Sc 3, inv-dec, sc 3] around—42 sc.

Rnd 31: [Sc 5, inv-dec] around—36 sc.

Rnd 32: [Sc 2, inv-dec, sc 2] around—30 sc.

Rnd 33: [Sc 3, inv-dec] around—24 sc.

Rnd 34: [Sc, inv-dec, sc] around—18 sc.

Rnd 35: Sc around.

Finish stuffing, paying close attention to stuffing tops of arms/shoulders firmly.

Fasten off B, change to A. Continue to Head.

HEAD

With A.

Rnd 1: Working in BLO, sc around—18 sc.

Place marker in last sc made to indicate end of rnd. Move marker up as each rnd is completed.

Rnd 2: 2 sc in each st around—36 sc.

Rnd 3: [Sc 5, 2 sc in next st] around—42 sc.

Rnd 4: [Sc 3, 2 sc in next st, sc 3] around—48 sc.

Rnd 5: [Sc 7, 2 sc in next st] around—54 sc.

Rnd 6: [Sc 4, 2 sc in next st, sc 4] around—60 sc.

Rnd 7: [Sc 9, 2 sc in next st] around—66 sc.

Rnds 8–21: Sc around.

Insert eyes in between Rnds 15 and 16, 12 sts apart. Before adding the safety backing, use white embroidery thread to add white detail to lower lid of eye, and black embroidery thread to add eyelashes. Using A, add nose detail between Rnds 12 and 13 over 3 sts.

Rnd 22: [Sc 9, inv-dec] around—60 sc.

Rnd 23: [Sc 4, inv-dec, sc 4] around—54 sc.

Rnd 24: [Sc 7, inv-dec] around—48 sc.

Rnd 25: [Sc 3, inv-dec, sc 3] around—42 sc.

Stuff Head and continue stuffing as work progresses.

Rnd 26: [Sc 5, inv-dec] around –36 sc.

Rnd 27: [Sc 2, inv-dec, sc 2] around—30 sc.

Rnd 28: [Sc, 3, inv-dec] around—24 sc.

Rnd 29: [Sc, inv-dec, sc] around—18 sc.

Rnd 30: [Sc, inv-dec] around—12 sc.

Rnd 31: Inv-dec around—6 sc.

Fasten off leaving a long tail for sewing; sew remaining 6 sts closed. Weave in ends.

EARS (MAKE 2)

With A.

Row 1: Ch 2, (3 sc, 3 hdc, sl st) in 2nd ch from hook—7 sts.

Fasten off, leaving a long tail for sewing.

HAIR CROWN

With E, work in BLO for entire piece.

Rnd 1: Ch 2, 6 sc in 2nd ch from hook—6 sc.

Place marker in last sc made to indicate end of rnd. Move marker up as each rnd is completed.

Rnd 2: 2 sc in each st around—12 sc.

Rnd 3: [2 sc, sc in next] around—18 sc.

Rnd 4: [Sc, 2 sc in next, sc in next] around—24 sc.

Rnd 5: [2 sc, sc in next 3] around—30 sc.

Rnd 6: [Sc 2, 2 sc in next, sc 2] around—36 sc.

Rnd 7: [2 sc, sc in next 5] around—42 sc.

Rnd 8: [Sc 3, 2 sc in next, sc 3] around—48 sc.

Rnd 9: [2 sc, sc in next 7] around—54 sc.

Rnd 10: [Sc 4, 2 sc in next, sc 4] around—60 sc.

Rnd 11: [2 sc, sc in next 9] around—66 sc.

Rnds 12–14: Sc around.

Begin working in turned rows.

Row 15: In BLO, sc 48, turn, leaving remaining 18 sts unworked—48 sc.

Row 16: Ch 1, sk 1st st, working in FLO across, sc 45, inv-dec, turn—45 sc.

Row 17: Ch 1, sk 1st st, working in BLO across, sc 42, inv-dec, turn—43 sc.

Row 18: Ch 1, sk 1st st, working in FLO across, sc 40, inv-dec, turn—41 sc.

Fasten off, leaving a long tail for sewing. Sew Hair Crown to top of head with 18 sts of Row 15 set at forehead, 7 rnds above edge of safety eyes. Sew Ears to each side of Head over edge of Hair Crown. Weave in ends.

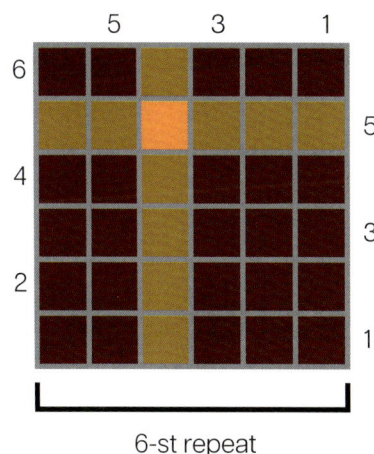

6-st repeat

KEY

- Mahogany (C)
- Ebony (F)
- Pumpkin (G)

HAIR

The hair for this doll is worked in 3 parts. The bangs are made first, then the long hair around the entire circumference of the Hair Crown, and finally 2 little pieces that sit in front of the ears at the side of the head.

BANGS

With E.

Hold doll facing away from you and work in FLO. Using two stitch markers, mark out 20 stitches across the center of the forehead of Rnd 11 of Hair Crown.

Row 1: Sl st to 1st marked st, [ch 6, sc in 2nd ch from hook and in next 4 ch, sl st in next 2 sts of Rnd 11 of Hair Crown] 9 times, ch 6, sc in 2nd ch from hook and in next 4 ch, sl st in next st—10 bang strands.

Fasten off, weave in ends. Secure center 6 strands of bangs to forehead by tacking them down using E. Leave 2 strands on each edge untacked/unsewn.

LONG HAIR

With E.

Rnd 1: Hold doll facing towards you and work in FLO, sl st to any st of Rnd 10 of Hair Crown behind bangs, [ch 41, sc in 2nd ch from hook, sc in next 39 ch, sl st in next 2 sts of Rnd 10 of Hair Crown] around the entire circumference of the Hair Crown.

Fasten off, weave in ends. Secure the first few inches of each strand of hair neatly to Hair Crown using E, and leaving the remainder of the strand untacked to braid with. Braid hair starting at the top center of the head and incorporating strands of hair as you work downwards. Secure braid with E. Weave in ends.

SIDE STRANDS

With E.

Row 1: Sl st to side of Hair Crown approximately 2 rnds lower than the edge of the bangs, ch 6, sc in 2nd ch from hook, sc in next 4 ch, sl st to Hair Crown.

Fasten off, weave in ends. Repeat for opposite side of head. Leave these strands of hair untacked/unsewn.

JACKET

The pieces of the Jacket are all worked in multiples of 6 sts and using the following color chart as a repeat. To use the color chart, work the 6 sts in the indicated colors of each row and repeat them across. Read RS rows of chart from right to left and WS rows from left to right.

Row 1: Ch 67, sc in 2nd ch from hook and in each ch across, turn—66 sc.

Rows 2–41: Ch 1 (does not count as a st here and throughout), sc across, turn.

SIDE A

The Jacket will be worked in 3 pieces to accommodate the arm holes, beginning with Side A which will decrease at the neckline. Follow the color chart for the decrease sections, eliminating the first st of each decrease section and maintaining the color chart as per the row below.

Row 1: Ch 1, sc, sc2tog, sc 13, turn; leave remaining 50 sts unworked—15 sc.

Row 2: Ch 1, sc across to last 2 sts, sc2tog, turn—14 sc.

Row 3: Ch 1, sc2tog, sc across, turn—13 sc.

Rows 4–5: Rep Rows 2–3—11 sts at end of Row 5.

Row 6: Rep Row 2—10 sc.

Fasten off, leaving a long tail for sewing.

MIDDLE OF BACK

Sk next 8 sts from last st of Row 1 of Side A. Join with a sl st.

Rows 1–6: Ch 1, sc 18, turn—18 sc.

Fasten off, weave in ends.

SIDE B

Sk next 8 sts from last st of Row 1 of Middle of Back. Join with a sl st.

Row 1: Ch 1, sc across to last 3 sts, sc2tog, sc in last, turn—15 sc.

Row 2: Ch 1, sc2tog, sc across, turn—14 sc.

Row 3: Ch 1, sc across to last 2 sts, sc2tog, turn—13 sc.

Rows 4–5: Rep Rows 2–3—11 sts at end of Row 5.

Row 6: Rep Row 2—10 sc.

Fasten off, leaving a long tail for sewing.

With Wrong Side of Jacket facing, sew shoulder seam for 3 sts on each side of Middle of Back to Sides A and B.

EDGING

With F, and right side facing, sc around entire jacket piece placing 1 sc in each st or row end. Fasten off, weave in ends.

COLLAR

The Collar uses Rows 3-6 of the color chart.

Row 1: Ch 31, sc in 2nd ch from hook and in each ch across, turn.

Rows 2–4: Ch 1, sc across, turn—30 sc.

Fasten off, leaving a long tail for sewing. Line up Collar with the center back of the jacket and sew collar around the top edge of the jacket. Weave in ends.

SLEEVES (MAKE 2)

Beginning with F and using color chart.

Row 1: Ch 19, sc in 2nd ch from hook, sc across, turn—18 sc.

Rows 2–16: Ch 1, sc across, turn.

Fasten off, leaving a long tail for sewing. With wrong side facing, sew row ends of sleeve together with seam. With wrong side of Jacket facing, insert sleeve end into sleeve hole and sew around entire sleeve edge to secure. Weave in ends.

FINISHING

Add 3 buttons to front of jacket.

"At some point,
you grow out of
being attracted to
that flame that burns
you over and over
and over again."

—TAYLOR SWIFT

"Cardigan" Sweater

Designed by Lee Sartori

Skill Level 1 2 3 **4**

When you reminisce about making someone feel better, was it something huge? A massive production? Or was it something small and meaningful? Oftentimes it's those little, seemingly insignificant acts of kindness that can ultimately make or break someone's entire day. A kind act as simple as a friendly smile, holding open a door, or an encouraging word can make all the difference in the world when someone is feeling down.

"Cardigan" is a song themed around taking care. It's noticing someone and meeting them exactly where they are and accepting them. It's about remembering a time when you needed help, only to have someone reach out a hand, and then being able to return that gesture to someone you love and who needs you, too. A warm hug and loving comfort.

Crochet this beautiful cardigan in a gorgeous cotton-blend yarn that features twisting cables on the front, back, and sleeves. And be sure to add the silver stars to the elbows for that extra bit of whimsy that will make this cardigan your favorite.

Size

XS (S, M, L, 1X, 2X, 3X, 4X, 5X)

Measurements

To fit bust: 28–30 (32–34, 36–38, 40–42, 44–46, 48–50, 52–54, 56–58, 60–62)" [81.5–86.5 (91.5–96.5, 101.5–106.5, 112–117, 122–127, 132–137, 142–147.5, 152.5–157.5) cm]

Actual bust: 30 (34, 38, 42, 46, 50, 54, 58, 62)" [76 (86.5, 96.5, 106.5, 117, 127, 137, 147.5, 157.5) cm]

Length: 19 (19, 20, 20, 21, 21, 21, 22, 22)" [48.5 (48.5, 51, 51, 53.5, 53.5, 53.5, 56, 56) cm]

Yarn

Worsted weight (#4 Medium)

Shown here: Lion Brand Made With Love The Cottony One, 185 yds (169 m), 3½ oz (100 g), 60% cotton, 40% acrylic: 8 (8, 9, 9, 10, 10, 11, 11, 12) balls 098 Lychee White (A), 1 ball each 152 Pewter Pan (B) and 105 Over The Moon (C)

Hooks

US size G/6 (4 mm) crochet hook, US size H/8 (5mm) crochet hook. Adjust hook size if necessary to obtain correct gauge.

Notions

3 medium black buttons

Yarn needle

3 stitch markers

Scissors

Gauge

16 hdc in BLO x 12 rows = 4" (10 cm) worked with larger hook.

Note

♥ Cardigan is worked in panels, beginning at the bottom of each panel with the hem.

Special Stitches

3rd FLO (front loop only): Half double crochet in the lower frontmost bar of the stitch only.

Bpdc (back post double crochet): Yarn over, insert the hook from back to front to back around the post of the stitch, yarn over and pull up a loop, [yarn over and pull through 2 loops] twice.

CONTINUED

Fpdc (front post double crochet): Yarn over, insert the hook from front to back to front around the post of the stitch, yarn over and pull up a loop, [yarn over and pull through 2 loops] twice.

Fptr (front post treble crochet): [Yarn over] twice, insert the hook from front to back to front around the post of the stitch, yarn over and pull up a loop, [yarn over and pull through 2 loops] 3 times.

Left Cross (worked over 6 sts): Sk next 3 sts, fptr around next 3 sts; working back over 3 skipped sts, fptr around each skipped st.

Pattern Stitch

Left Cable (worked over 14 sts)

Row 1 (RS): Fpdc around next 2 sts, bpdc around next 2 sts, fpdc around next 6 sts, bpdc around next 2 sts, fpdc around next 2 sts.

Row 2: Bpdc around next 2 sts, fpdc around next 2 sts, bpdc around next 6 sts, fpdc around next 2 sts, bpdc around next 2 sts.

Row 3: Fpdc around next 2 sts, bpdc around next 2 sts, work Left Cross over next 6 sts, bpdc around next 2 sts, fpdc around next 2 sts.

Row 4: Rep Row 2.

Rep Rows 1–4 for Left Cable pattern.

TAYLOR-MADE FOR YOU

Crochet cables can seem intimidating, but breaking them down to only 6 stitches makes them a breeze! Enjoy the twisting cables on this beautiful cardigan.

BACK PANEL

Hem

With smaller crochet hook and A.

Row 1: Ch 6, sc in 2nd ch from hook and in each ch across, turn—5 sc.

Rows 2–60 (68, 76, 84, 92, 100, 108, 116, 124): Ch 1, working in BLO, sc across, turn.

Do not fasten off.

Body

With larger crochet hook and A.

Row 1: Ch 1, rotate to work in row ends, sc in each row end across, turn—60 (68, 76, 84, 92, 100, 108, 116, 124) sc.

Fasten off A, change to B.

Rows 2–3: Ch 1, sc in each st across, turn.

Change to A.

Rows 4–5: Ch 1, sc across, turn.

Change to B.

Rows 6–7: Ch 1, sc across, turn.

Fasten off B, change to A.

Row 8: Ch 1, hdc across, turn.

Cable Pattern

Row 9 (RS): Ch 1, working in BLO, hdc in next 8 (10, 12, 14, 16, 18, 20, 22, 24) sts; work Row 1 of Left Cable pattern; working in BLO, hdc in next 16 (20, 24, 28, 32, 36, 40, 44, 48) sts; work Row 1 of Left Cable pattern; working in BLO, hdc in next 8 (10, 12, 14, 16, 18, 20, 22, 24) sts, turn—60 (68, 76, 84, 92, 100, 108, 116, 124) sts.

Row 10: Ch 1, working in 3rd FLO, hdc in next 8 (10, 12, 14, 16, 18, 20, 22, 24) sts; work Row 2 of Left Cable pattern; working in 3rd FLO, hdc in next 16 (20, 24, 28, 32, 36, 40, 44, 48) sts; work Row 2 of Left Cable pattern; working in 3rd FLO, hdc in next 8 (10, 12, 14, 16, 18, 20, 22, 24) sts, turn.

Row 11: Ch 1, working in BLO, hdc in next 8 (10, 12, 14, 16, 18, 20, 22, 24) sts; work Row 3 of Left Cable pattern; working in BLO, hdc in next 16 (20, 24, 28, 32, 36, 40, 44, 48) sts; work Row 3 of Left Cable pattern; working in BLO, hdc in next 8 (10, 12, 14, 16, 18, 20, 22, 24) sts, turn.

Row 12: Ch 1, working in 3rd FLO, hdc in next 8 (10, 12, 14, 16, 18, 20, 22, 24) sts; work Row 4 of Left Cable pattern; working in 3rd FLO, hdc in next 16 (20, 24, 28, 32, 36, 40, 44, 48) sts; work Row 4 of Left Cable; working in 3rd FLO, hdc in next 8 (10, 12, 14, 16, 18, 20, 22, 24) sts, turn.

Remaining Body Rows: Rep Rows 9–12 until Back Panel measures approximately 19 (19, 20, 20, 21, 21, 21, 22, 22)" [48.5 (48.5, 51, 51, 53.5, 53.5, 53.5, 56, 56) cm] from beg, ending in a RS row.

Edging

With larger hook and A.

Row 1: With RS of panel facing, and continuing from top left corner, ch 1 and rotate to work in row ends, sc in each row end to bottom. Fasten off.

Row 2: With RS of panel facing, join to bottom right corner of panel with a sl st, ch 1, sc in each row end to top of shoulder. Fasten off.

RIGHT FRONT PANEL

Hem

With smaller crochet hook and A.

Row 1: Ch 6, sc in 2nd ch from hook and in each ch across, turn—5 sc.

Rows 2–30 (34, 38, 42, 46, 50, 54, 58, 62): Ch 1, working in BLO, sc across, turn.

Do not fasten off, continue to body.

Body

With larger crochet hook and A.

Rows 1–8: Work same as Rows 1–8 of back panel, working over 30 (34, 38, 42, 46, 50, 54, 58, 62) sc.

Cable Pattern

Row 9 (RS): Ch 1, working in BLO, hdc 3; fpdc around next 6 sts; working in BLO, hdc across, turn.

Row 10: Ch 1, working in FLO, hdc in each st to last 9 sts; bpdc around next 6 sts; working in FLO, hdc 3, turn.

Row 11: Ch 1, working in BLO, hdc 3; work Left Cross; working in BLO, hdc across, turn.

Row 12: Rep Row 10.

Remaining Body Rows: Rep Rows 9-12 until Right Front Panel measures approximately 12 (12, 13, 13, 14, 14, 14, 15, 15)" [30.5 (30.5, 33, 33, 35.5, 35.5, 35.5, 38, 38) cm], ending in a WS row.

Neckline Decrease

Row 1 (RS): Ch 1, working in BLO, hdc 3; work in established cable pattern over next 6 sts; working in BLO, hdc2tog (place marker), hdc across, turn—29 (33, 37, 41, 45, 49, 53, 57, 61) sts.

Row 2: Ch 1, working in FLO, hdc in each hdc to 2 sts before marked st, hdc2tog; work in established cable pattern over next 6 sts; working in FLO, hdc 3, turn—28 (32, 36, 40, 44, 48, 52, 56, 60) sts.

Rows 3–21: Rep Rows 1–2—9 (13, 17, 21, 25, 29, 33, 37, 41) sts remaining after Row 21.

LEFT FRONT PANEL

Hem

With smaller crochet hook and A.

Row 1: Ch 6, sc in 2nd ch from hook and in each ch across, turn—5 sc.

Rows 2–30 (34, 38, 42, 46, 50, 54, 58, 62): Ch 1, working in BLO, sc across, turn.

Do not fasten off, continue to body.

Body

With larger crochet hook and A.

Rows 1–8: Work same as Rows 1–8 of back, working over 30 (34, 38, 42, 46, 50, 54, 58, 62) sc.

Cable Pattern

Row 9 (RS): Ch 1, working in BLO, hdc across to last 9 sts; fpdc around next 6 sts; working in BLO, hdc 3, turn.

Row 10: Ch 1, working in FLO, hdc 3; bpdc around next 6 sts; working in FLO, hdc 21 (25, 29, 33, 37, 41, 45, 49, 53), turn.

Row 11: Ch 1, working in BLO, hdc to last 9 sts; work Left Cross; working in BLO, hdc 3, turn.

Row 12: Rep Row 10.

Remaining Body Rows: Rep Rows 9–12 until Left Front Panel measures approximately 12 (12, 13, 13, 14, 14, 14, 15, 15)" [30.5 (30.5, 33, 33, 35.5, 35.5, 35.5, 38, 38) cm], ending in a WS row.

Neckline Decrease

Row 1 (RS): Ch 1, working in BLO, hdc across to last 10 sts, hdc2tog (place marker), work in established cable pattern over next 6 sts; working in BLO, hdc 3, turn—29 (33, 37, 41, 45, 49, 53, 57, 61) sts.

Row 2: Ch 1, working in FLO, hdc 3; work in established cable pattern over next 6 sts; working in FLO, hdc2tog, hdc across, turn—28 (32, 36, 40, 44, 48, 52, 56, 60) sts.

Rows 3–21: Rep Rows 1–2—9 (13, 17, 21, 25, 29, 33, 37, 41) sts remaining after Row 21.

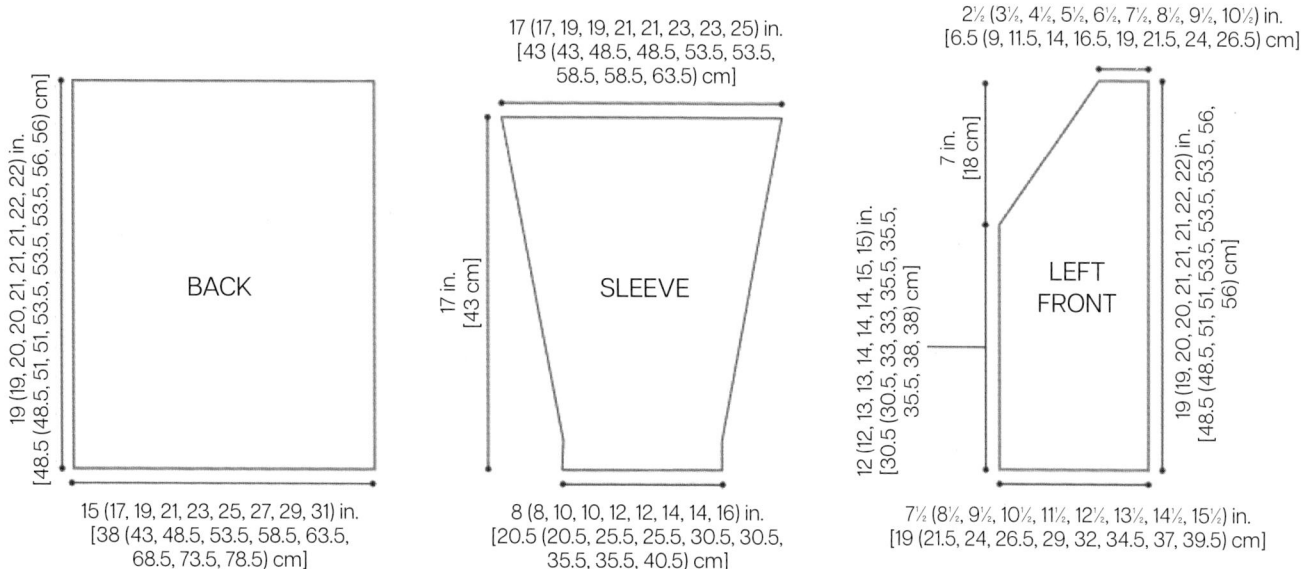

Schematic Measurements

BACK

19 (19, 20, 20, 21, 21, 21, 22, 22) in.
[48.5 (48.5, 51, 51, 53.5, 53.5, 53.5, 56, 56) cm]

15 (17, 19, 21, 23, 25, 27, 29, 31) in.
[38 (43, 48.5, 53.5, 58.5, 63.5, 68.5, 73.5, 78.5) cm]

SLEEVE

17 (17, 19, 19, 21, 21, 23, 23, 25) in.
[43 (43, 48.5, 48.5, 53.5, 53.5, 58.5, 58.5, 63.5) cm]

17 in.
[43 cm]

8 (8, 10, 10, 12, 12, 14, 14, 16) in.
[20.5 (20.5, 25.5, 25.5, 30.5, 30.5, 35.5, 35.5, 40.5) cm]

LEFT FRONT

2½ (3½, 4½, 5½, 6½, 7½, 8½, 9½, 10½) in.
[6.5 (9, 11.5, 14, 16.5, 19, 21.5, 24, 26.5) cm]

7 in.
[18 cm]

12 (12, 13, 13, 14, 14, 14, 15, 15) in.
[30.5 (30.5, 33, 33, 35.5, 35.5, 35.5, 38, 38) cm]

19 (19, 20, 20, 21, 21, 21, 22, 22) in.
[48.5 (48.5, 51, 51, 53.5, 53.5, 53.5, 56, 56) cm]

7½ (8½, 9½, 10½, 11½, 12½, 13½, 14½, 15½) in.
[19 (21.5, 24, 26.5, 29, 32, 34.5, 37, 39.5) cm]

SLEEVE (MAKE 2)

Hem

With smaller crochet hook and A.

Row 1: Ch 6, sc in 2nd ch from hook and in each ch across, turn—5 sc.

Rows 2–32 (32, 40, 40, 48, 48, 56, 56, 64): Ch 1, working in BLO, sc across, turn.

Do not fasten off.

Body

With larger hook and A.

Rows 1–8: Work same as Rows 1-8 of back panel, working over 32 (32, 40, 40, 48, 48, 56, 56, 64) sc.

Cable Pattern

Row 9 (RS): Ch 1, working in BLO, hdc 9 (9, 13, 13, 17, 17, 21, 21, 25); work Row 1 of Left Cable pattern; working in BLO, hdc 9 (9, 13, 13, 17, 17, 21, 21, 25), turn—32 (32, 40, 40, 48, 48, 56, 56, 64) sts.

Row 10: Ch 1, working in FLO, 2 hdc in 1st st, hdc across to the 14 Left Cable pattern sts; work Row 2 of Left Cable pattern; working in FLO, hdc across to last st, 2 hdc in last st, turn—34 (34, 42, 42, 50, 50, 58, 58, 66) sts.

Row 11: Ch 1, working in BLO, hdc across to the 14 Left Cable pattern sts; work Row 3 of Left Cable pattern; working in BLO, hdc across, turn.

Row 12: Ch 1, working in FLO, 2 hdc in 1st st, hdc across to the 14 Left Cable pattern sts; work Row 4 of Left Cable pattern; working in FLO, hdc across to last st, 2 hdc in last st, turn—36 (36, 44, 44, 52, 52, 60, 60, 68) sts.

Row 13: Ch 1, working in BLO, hdc across to the 14 Left Cable pattern sts; work Row 1 of Left Cable pattern; working in BLO, hdc across, turn.

Row 14–45: Rep Rows 10–13—68 (68, 76, 76, 84, 84, 92, 92, 100) sts at end of Row 45.

Row 46: Ch 1, working in FLO, hdc across to the 14 Left Cable pattern sts; work Row 2 of Left Cable pattern; working in FLO, hdc across turn.

Row 47: Ch 1, sc in each st across.

Fasten off.

ASSEMBLY

With A and WS facing, use preferred joining method (I used sc to join, but sewing works as well) to join shoulder seams of front and back panel on left and right side.

Lay panels open on a flat surface and insert sleeves on each side of cardigan, centering the middle top of the sleeve to the join of the shoulder seam. Join sleeve to panels.

With WS facing and with front panels atop back panel, seam from wrist to armpit, and from armpit to bottom hem.

Weave in ends.

FRONT AND NECK BANDS

With RS facing, A and larger hook.

Join to bottom right panel with a sl st.

Row 1 (RS): Ch 1, sc evenly across row ends along edge of right panel up to neckline, across neckline, and down left panel.

Change to B.

Rows 2–8: Ch 1, sc in each st across, turn AND change yarn color as follows: Work first 2 rows with B, 2 rows with A, 2 rows with B, and last row with A.

Do not fasten off.

RIBBING

With A and smaller hook.

With 3 locking stitch markers, mark buttonholes along right front. Place 1st st marker approximately 1" (2.5 cm) from bottom. Place 3rd stitch marker approximately halfway up the panel, right where the decreases begin and the neckline begins to taper. Place the 2nd stitch marker evenly between the 1st and 3rd marker. These will mark where you will complete the buttonholes while crocheting the ribbing.

Complete Ribbing Rows until you reach a stitch marker. When you reach a stitch marker, complete Buttonhole Rows.

RIBBING ROWS

Row 1 (RS): Ch 6, sc in 2nd ch from hook and in each ch, sl st in next 2 sts of Row 8 of collar, turn—5 sc.

Row 2: Ch 1, sk 2 sl sts, working in BLO, sc 5, turn.

Row 3: Ch 1, working in BLO, sc 5, sl st in next 2 sts of Row 8 of Collar, turn.

Rep Rows 2–3, ending with a RS row (Row 3).

BUTTONHOLE ROWS

Row 1 (WS): Ch 1, sk 2 sl sts, working in BLO, sc 5, turn.

Row 2: Ch 1, working in BLO, sc, ch 3, sk next 3 sts (buttonhole made), sc in last, sl st in next 2 sts of Row 8 of collar, turn.

Row 3: Ch 1, sk 2 sl sts, working in BLO, sc in 1st sc, sc in next 3 ch, sc in last, turn.

Row 4: Ch 1, working in BLO, sc in next 5 sts, sl st in next 2 sts of Row 8 of collar, turn.

Return to Ribbing Rows 2–3.

STARS (MAKE 6)

With C and smaller hook.

Rnd 1: Ch 2, 5 sc in 2nd ch from hook—5 sc.

Rnd 2: 2 sc in each st around—10 sc.

Rnd 3: 2 sc, sc in next st around—15 sc.

Rnd 4: *Ch 4, sc in 2nd ch from hook, hdc in next ch, dc in next ch, skip next st on working round, sl st in next 2 sts; rep from * around, join—5 points made.

Fasten off leaving a long tail for sewing.

FINISHING

Using 3 stitch markers, close front of cardigan and match the 3 buttonholes to the opposite side ribbing. Place a stitch marker where each button will line up with buttonhole.

Sew buttons to opposite side ribbing of buttonholes.

Sew Stars to sleeve by first laying sleeve flat and working on the back half at the elbow. Place 3 stars near each other at elbow over approximately 12 rows each. Sew stars to sleeve, fasten off, and weave in ends.

Weave in all ends.

"Marjorie" Granny Square Blanket

Designed by Lee Sartori

I am one of those exceptionally lucky individuals who had many wonderful years with my grandmother. My grandma was my person, one of the great loves of my life. I am extremely grateful to have shared so many special moments with her and I miss her terribly.

When I first heard "Marjorie," I completely understood the feeling of loss. I can wholeheartedly appreciate what it means to never get the chance to create those special memories with someone so important in life.

"Marjorie" takes me on a journey of what it means to find the beauty in loss. This sorrowful ballad captures the emotions that come with love, death, and grief. The "Marjorie," blanket represents all the memories we hold dear to our hearts. It's made with a classic crochet stitch appropriately called "the Granny Square" and with the colors that Taylor wore for her performances during the Eras Tour. It's reminiscent of amber skies, frozen swims, and sparkles. The finished blanket is made with chunky and soft yarn that will wrap you up in a warm embrace. It is the perfect memory keeper.

Measurements

69" (175.5 cm) wide x 87" (221 cm) long

Yarn

Chunky weight (#5 Bulky)

Shown here: Lion Brand Basic Stitch Anti-Microbial Thick & Quick, 87 yds (79.5 m), 3½ oz (100 g), 65% recycled polyester, 35% acrylic: 19 balls 152 Charcoal (A), 16 balls 178 Maize (B), 4 balls 106 Bluestone (C)

Hook

US size M/13 (9.0 mm) crochet hook. Adjust hook size if necessary to obtain correct gauge.

Notions

Yarn needle

Stitch marker

Scissors

Gauge

Gauge is not critical for this project.

1 square = 6" x 6" (15 x 15 cm)

Skill Level

1 **2** 3 4

Notes

♥ Each blanket square is worked in turned rows.

♥ Blanket is made using "join as you go" method for joining squares in the final round of the pattern. You can find many helpful video tutorials online for this technique. Alternatively, you can use traditional seaming methods to join your squares.

♥ Border is added after assembled blanket is complete.

Special Stitches

Join Cluster St: To join two squares together for the border, complete a dc in the 1st corner, dc2tog over the 1st and 2nd corner, and dc in the 2nd corner (new cluster made).

CONTINUED

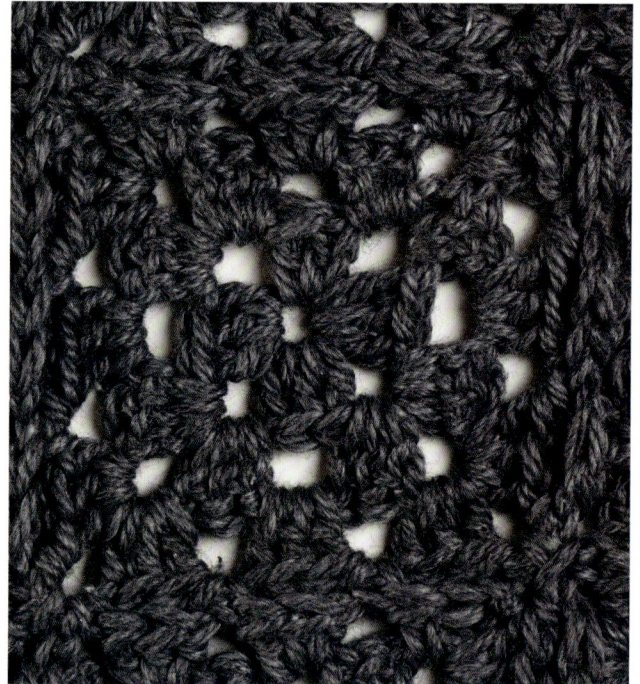

BLANKET SQUARE (MAKE 154—84 WITH A AND 70 WITH B)

Rnd 1: Ch 4, 2 dc in 4th ch from hook (3 skipped ch count as dc), ch 2, *(3 dc, ch 2) in same ch; rep from * 3 times, join with sl st in top of beg ch, turn—12 dc, 4 ch-2 spaces.

Rnd 2: Ch 3 (counts as dc), 2 dc in 1st ch-2 space, *ch 1, (3 dc, ch 2, 3 dc) in next ch-2 space; rep from * to 1st ch-2 space, ch 1, 3 dc in 1st ch-2 space, ch 2, join, turn—24 dc, 4 ch-1 spaces, and 4 ch-2 spaces.

Rnd 3: Ch 3, 2 dc in 1st ch-2 space, *ch 1, 3 dc in next ch-1 space, ch 1, (3 dc, ch 2, 3 dc) in next ch-2 space; rep from * to last ch-1 space, ch 1, 3 dc in last ch-1 space, ch 1, 3 dc in 1st ch-2 space, ch 2, join, turn—36 dc, 8 ch-1 spaces, and 4 ch-2 spaces.

Fasten off.

ASSEMBLY

Arrange squares following layout diagram and crochet or sew squares together.

BORDER

With C.

With RS facing, join to top left corner in the ch-2 space.

Rnd 1: Ch 3, 2 dc in same space, *[(ch 1, 3 dc) in next ch-1 space across to where 2 squares meet, ch 1, [Join Cluster St] across to corner ch-2 space of blanket, (ch 1, 3 dc, ch 2, 3 dc) in corner space; rep from * around, ch 1, (3 dc, ch 2) in beginning ch-2 space, join.

Rnd 2: Ch 3, 2 dc in same space, *[sc in center dc of next 3-dc group, 5 dc in next ch-1 space] across to next ch-2 corner space, (3 dc, ch 2, 3 dc) in corner ch-2 space; rep from * around, 3 dc in beginning ch-2 space, ch 2, join.

Fasten off, weave in ends.

FINISHING

Weave in all ends.

TAYLOR-MADE FOR YOU

Spend less time sewing by joining your Granny Squares together with the "join as you go" method.

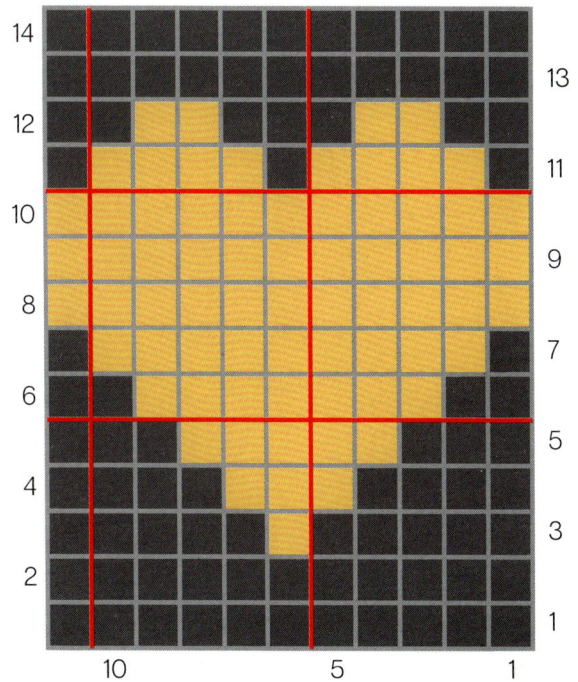

KEY

■ A-colored Blanket Square
■ B-colored Blanket Square

"Most of my songs have names of people I've met or are dear to me. There are people who have privacy issues and about people knowing about their private life. But for me, I like to include few special names and few details about them to make the song very special to me."

—TAYLOR SWIFT

"All Too Well" Scarf

Skill Level
1 2 3 4

Designed by Lee Sartori

When can a scarf be more than "just a scarf"? Sometimes a scarf can serve as a poignant symbol, resurrecting the bittersweet memories of a past relationship and everything associated with it. Sometimes stitched into a simple scarf, we add the weight of shared experiences, longing, and even retrospection. Sometimes a scarf isn't just a scarf, it is also an act of healing through the motion of each and every stitch made. The time we take to crochet a scarf echoes the passage of time and the lingering thoughts of a lost connection. The texture carries the tactile history of emotions woven into the fabric. A scarf can become the emblem of heartache, a silent witness to the intensity of everything we're feeling. That's when a scarf can become more than "just a scarf."

We know all too well that you've made lots of scarves in your history as a crocheter, but I invite you to find your favorite red yarn and crochet an absolutely gorgeous texture (called Alpine stitch), row by row. As you stitch, I hope you find calm, peace, and healing along the journey down whatever road you may travel.

Size

One size

Measurements

12" (30.5 cm) wide x 52" (132 cm) long

Yarn

Worsted weight (#4 Medium)

Shown here: Lion Brand Basic Stitch Anti-Pilling, 185 yds (169 m), 3½ oz (100 g), 100% acrylic: 5 balls 400 Red Heather

Hook

US Size G/6 (4.0 mm) crochet hook. Adjust hook size if necessary to obtain correct gauge.

Notions

Yarn needle

Scissors

Gauge

Gauge is not critical for this project.

17 sts x 13 rows in pattern repeat = 4" (10 cm)

Notes

♥ The scarf is worked in turned rows, width-wise.

♥ Fringe is added at the end of the pattern.

♥ Long fpdc takes the place of a stitch in the working row.

Special Stitches

Long fpdc (long front post double crochet): Yo, insert hook from front to back around dc 2 rows below, yo and draw up a loop to height of working row, [yo and draw through 2 loops] twice.

CONTINUED

TAYLOR-MADE FOR YOU

One of my favorite things about scarf patterns is how versatile they can be. Turn your "All Too Well" Scarf into an infinity scarf by omitting the fringe and sewing the short ends together for a different look!

SCARF

Row 1 (WS): Ch 51, sc in 2nd ch from hook and in each ch across, turn—50 sc.

Row 2 (RS): Ch 3 (counts as a st here and throughout), dc across, turn—50 dc.

Pattern repeat begins.

Row 3: Ch 1 (does not count as a st here and throughout), sc across, turn.

Row 4: Ch 3, [dc in next st of working row, long fpdc around next st] across to last st, dc in last st of working row, turn—50 sts.

Row 5: Rep Row 3.

Row 6: Ch 3, [long fpdc around next st, dc in next st of working row] across to last st, dc in last st of working row, turn—50 sts.

Rows 7–174: Rep Rows 3–6.

Row 175: Rep Row 3.

BORDER

With RS facing, ch 1, rotate to work across row ends, sc in each row end, ch 2, rotate to work across underside of foundation ch, sc in each ch across, ch 2, rotate to work across row ends, sc in each row end, ch 2, sc across Row 175, ch 2 and join with slip st in first sc—450 sc, 4 ch-2 spaces.

Weave in all ends.

FINISHING

Cut approximately 100 pieces of yarn measuring 8" long. Add a piece of fringe to each st of short ends of scarf by looping folded piece of fringe through the stitch and cinching the tails through the loop to secure.

"You have people come into your life shockingly and surprisingly. You have losses that you never thought you'd experience. You have rejection and you have to learn how to deal with that and how to get up the next day and go on with it."

—TAYLOR SWIFT

CHAPTER *Three*

DELIGHT

"I have this really high priority on happiness and finding something to be happy about."

—TAYLOR SWIFT

As crocheters, we all know that warm and fuzzy feeling that comes when we finish a new crochet project. Or buy yarn for a new crochet project. Or start a new crochet project! This chapter is filled with all the delightful things that you could hope to make! The "22" Knee-High Socks are so fun and fancy! The "Shake It Off" Beanie is the ultimate gift. And if you're a big Swiftie, you'll be delighted by the "Karma" Cat Bag because it might be the cutest thing in this book!

"Shake It Off" Beanie

Designed by Meghan Ballmer

Skill Level
1 2 **3** 4

We all have bad days. Those days where you just don't want to get out of your warm bed in the morning, and when all the little things that can go wrong do. There are days when you feel like you don't fit in for one reason or another and that no matter how hard you try you never will. But what you may not see right now, and what some people may never see, are all the things that you have to be proud of. You're unique! One of a kind. And you've done some fantastic things.

"Shake It Off" was written as the perfect mantra to get through the day with a smile and embrace your differences. This song is a hug and a friendly reminder that everything is going to be okay.

As Swift said on her official YouTube channel, "I've learned a pretty tough lesson that people can say whatever they want about us at any time, and we cannot control that. The only thing we can control is our reaction to that."

The "Shake It Off" beanie is a nod to the cheerleader outfit Taylor Swift wears in the music video for the song. When you crochet one and get cozy in it, I hope it reminds you of how amazing you are, and that it helps you stay upbeat and positive! And remember, who cares what people say!

Size

Tween (Adult)

Measurements

Finished circumference: 17 (19)" [43 (48.5) cm]

Finished height: 9 (9.5)" [23 (24) cm], with brim folded up and not including pom-pom

Yarn

DK weight (#3 Light)

Shown here: Lion Brand LB Collection Superwash Merino, 306 yds (279 m), 3½ oz (100 g), 100% extra fine wool: 1 ball each of 098 Antique (A), 111 Midnight Blue (B), 158 Mustard Seed (C)

Hook

US size E/4 (3.5 mm) crochet hook. Adjust hook size if necessary to obtain correct gauge.

Notions

Yarn needle

Stitch marker

Scissors

Pom-pom maker (optional)

Gauge

20 sts x 25 rows in sc in the round = 4" (10 cm)

Notes

♥ Hat is worked in joined rounds entirely in single crochet.

♥ After Rnd 37 you will fold the hat in half in order to create the double brim.

♥ Use the intarsia crochet technique to create the "TS." Separate B and C into 4-5 small balls of yarn and do not carry those colors throughout the rounds. Work around A strand using the tapestry crochet technique. Use the chart as a reference. All rounds are read from right to left.

Special Stitches

Fsc (foundation single crochet): Ch 2, insert hook in 2nd ch from hook and pull up loop, yo and pull through 1 loop (ch made), yo and pull through 2 loops (sc made), *insert hook in ch of previous st and pull up loop, yo and pull through 1 loop (ch made), yo and pull through 2 loops (sc made); rep from * for required number of fsc.

CONTINUED

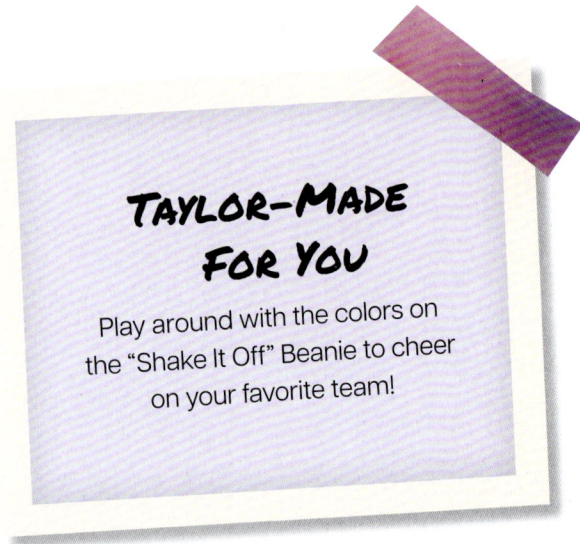

TAYLOR-MADE FOR YOU

Play around with the colors on the "Shake It Off" Beanie to cheer on your favorite team!

HAT

Rnd 1: With A, Fsc 85 (95) sts; bring the beginning st to the last st, making sure not to twist the sts, and join with sl st.

Rnd 2: Ch 1, sc in each st around, join—85 (95) sts.

Change to B, do not fasten off A. Carry both colors up the seam as you go.

Rnds 3 and 4: Ch 1, sc in each st around, join.

Change to A.

Rnds 5 and 6: Ch 1, sc in each st around, join.

Change to B.

Rnds 7–37: Rep Rnds 3-6, continuing to change yarn color every 2 rnds, ending with a Rnd 5.

Cut B. Work remainder of beanie with A.

Fold the piece in half so the beginning round and current round are together and WS are touching.

Rnd 38: Ch 1, sc the current round and the bottom sts of round 1 together all the way around—85 (95) sts.

Rnds 39–54: Ch 1, sc in each st around, join—85 (95) sts.

CHARTED INITIALS

Place markers in the 32nd (37th) and 57th (62nd) sts to indicate the first and last st for the "TS" pattern. Move markers up as each rnd is completed.

Rnd 1: Ch 1, with A, sc in each st to first marked st; sc in each st to next marker AND change yarn color following Row 1 of chart; with A, sc in each st to end, join.

Rnds 2–20: With A, ch 1, sc in each st to first marked st; sc in each st to next marker AND change yarn color following next row of chart; with A, sc in each st to end, join.

Cut B and C. Work remainder of beanie with A only.

Rnds 21–37 (39): Ch 1, sc in each st around, join.

Fasten off, leaving a long tail for seaming.

FINISHING

Using a yarn needle and the long tail, fold hat in half and make one stitch going though both sides in the center. Fold hat in half the other way and make one stitch going through center of both sides and middle of hat. You will now have four "loops" at the top of your hat. Stitch the middle of each of those "loops" to the center stitch of the hat. You will now have 8 small "loops" at the top of your hat. Stitch the middle of each of those "loops" to the center stitch of the hat to close. Bring the tail to the inside of the hat and tie and knot. Weave in all ends.

Optional: Use the remaining yarn and a pom-pom maker to make a large pom-pom. Attach to the top of the hat and secure with a knot inside.

Fold double brim up.

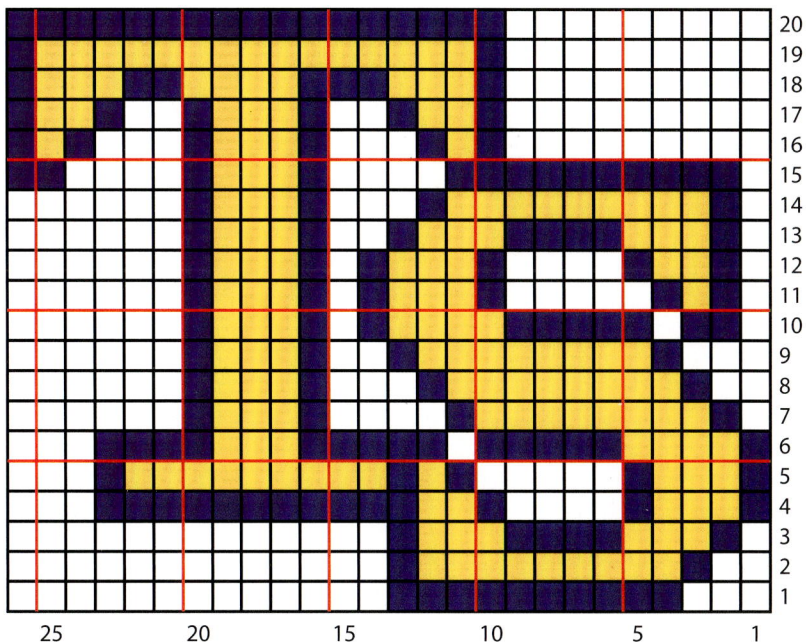

KEY

- ☐ Antique (A)
- ■ Midnight Blue (B)
- ▨ Mustard Seed (C)

"I think the tiniest little thing can change the course of your day, which can change the course of your year, which can change who you are."

—TAYLOR SWIFT

"Anything you put your mind to and add your imagination into can make your life a lot better and a lot more fun."

—TAYLOR SWIFT

"22" Knee-High Socks

Designed by Julie Desjardins

It's time to hike up your knee-high socks and dance the night away! We all have memories of those perfect times with amazing friends. Nights filled with laughter, fun, and excitement! It's silly things like waffles at midnight, movie marathons, or heading out on the town and hopping from place to place. When you're with your friends, it's easy to forget about work, or school, or even heartbreaks. Everything will be okay because you're together! Taylor told *Billboard Magazine*: "For me, being 22 has been my favorite year of my life. I like all the possibilities of how you're still learning, but you know enough. You still know nothing, but you know that you know nothing. You're old enough to start planning your life, but you're young enough to know there are so many unanswered questions. That brings about a carefree feeling that is sort of based on indecision and fear and at the same time letting loose. Being 22 has taught me so much."

The "22" socks are the perfect accessory to pair with some black shorts and your favorite white t-shirt, and don't forget the heart-shaped sunnies!

Size

XS (S, M, L, XL)

To fit: US shoe size Youth 4–6 (Women's 4–6½, Women's 7–9½/Men's 6–8½, Women's 10–12½/Men's 9–11½, Men's 10–12½)

Measurements

Foot circumference: 7 (7, 8, 9, 10)" [18 (18, 20.5, 23, 25.5) cm]

Foot length: 10 (9½, 10, 10½, 12)" [25.5 (24, 25.5, 26.5, 30.5) cm]

Sock height: 21 (23, 24½, 27, 29¾)" [53.5 (58.5, 62, 68.5, 75.5) cm], over the knee

Yarn

DK weight (#3 Light)

Shown here: Lion Brand FeelsLike Heaven, 246 yds (224 m), 3½ oz (100 g), 100% nylon: 3 balls 100 White (A)

Worsted weight (#4 Medium)

Shown here: Lion Brand Basic Stitch Anti-Piling, 185 yds (169 m), 3½ oz (100 g), 100% acrylic: 1 ball each 153 Black (B), and 400 Red Heather (C)

Hook

US Size I/9 (5.5 mm) crochet hook. Adjust hook size if necessary to obtain correct gauge.

Notions

Yarn needle

2 stitch markers (in different colors)

Scissors

Measuring tape

Row counter

2 lengths of white satin ribbon, 2 yds (1.8 m) long x 0.4" (1 cm) wide

Gauge

16 sts x 16 rows in single crochet = 4" (10 cm)

Notes

♥ Socks are worked toe up, with a common heel.

♥ Adjust foot length or sock height: each 2-row rep adds or subtracts ½" (1.27 cm) to the foot length or height of the sock.

CONTINUED

TAYLOR-MADE FOR YOU

Try on your socks as you go to make sure they are the perfect length for your legs! You can omit rows from the top for the best fit.

SOCK (MAKE 2)

Toe

With A. Working in continuous rounds.

Rnd 1 (RS): Ch 11, sc in 2nd ch from hook and in each ch across, pivot your work to crochet under sts just made, sc in each st across, do not join in this section—20 sts.

Place a stitch marker in first and eleventh sts. Move markers up into first st of both increases each round.

Rnds 2–3 (3, 4, 5, 6): [2 sc in next st, sc in each st until 1 st before next marker, 2 sc in next st] twice—28 (28, 32, 36, 40) sts.

Rnds 4–5 (4–5, 5–7, 6–9, 7–11): Sc in each st around.

At the end of the last round, sl st in first st.

Tip: Lay Toe flat. If first stitch is not at the edge of the sock, sc around to st just before edge and sl st in next st. Your next round will begin here.

Foot

Working in joined, turned rounds.

Odd-numbered rounds are on the RS, even-numbered rounds are on the WS throughout.

Rnd 1 (RS): Ch 1, sc-BLO in each st around, join with a sl st in first sc, turn.

Rnds 2–24 (22, 22, 22, 26): Ch 1, sc in each st around, join with a sl st in first sc, turn.

Gusset

Next rnd (RS): Ch 1, sc in next 14 (14, 16, 18, 20) sts for top of foot, 2 sc in next sc, place a marker in the first sc of 2-sc group just made, sc in next 12 (12, 14, 16, 18) sts, 2 sc in next st for bottom of foot, join with a sl st in first sc, turn—30 (30, 34, 38, 42) sts.

Next 2 rnds: Ch 1, sc in each st to marker, 2 sc in marked st and move marker to first sc of 2-sc group just made, sc in each st across to last st 2 sc in last st, join—34 (34, 38, 42, 46) sts.

Heel

Heel is worked back and forth in rows.

Rows 1–11: Ch 1, sc in each st across, turn.

At the end of the last row, fasten off, leaving a long tail to sew the heel closed.

Match the 17 (17, 19, 21, 23) sts of both halves of last heel row. Sewing through both thicknesses, sew the matching sts together for back of heel—17 (17, 19, 21, 23) sts.

Leg

With RS facing, join yarn at seam with a sl st to work in joined, turned rounds.

Rnd 1 (RS): Ch 1, sc in 11 row ends of heel, sc across top of foot sts, sc in 11 row ends of heel, join with sl st in first sc, turn—36 (36, 38, 40, 42) sts.

Next 3 (3, 2, 1, 0) row(s): Ch 1, sc in next st, sc2tog, sc in each st to last 3 sts, sc2tog, sc in last st, join with a sl st in first sc, turn—30 (30, 34, 38, 42) sts.

Tip: If you have larger ankles, disregard the decreases, working evenly instead.

Next rnd: Ch 1, sc in each st around, join with a sl st in first sc, turn.

Rep last rnd until there are a total of 25 rnds in leg.

Rnd 26: Ch 1, (sc, ch 3, sc) in first st (bottom loop made), sc in each st around, join with a sl st in first sc, turn—31 (31, 35, 39, 43) sts and 1 ch-3 space.

Work now progresses back and forth in rows.

Row 27: Ch 1, sc in each st to ch-3 of bottom loop; leave remaining sts unworked, turn—30 (30, 34, 38, 42) sts.

Rows 28 and 29: Ch 4 (edge loop made), sc in each st across; leave the ch-4 edge loop unworked, turn.

Rows 30 and 31: Ch 1, sc in each sc across; leave the ch-4 edge loop unworked, turn.

Rep Rows 28–31 and AT THE SAME TIME, work 2 sc in 3rd st of every 5th row, starting with Row 32, until you have 35 (37, 42, 45, 53) sts, then continue to rep Rows 28-31 without any increasing for a total of 59 (67, 71, 79, 87) rows in the leg.

If you do not want lace at the top of the sock, proceed to the Plain Top instructions.

TOP LACE

With B.

Next row: Ch 1, sc in 1st sc, ch 5, *sc in next 5 sts, ch 5, rep from * to last st, sc in last st and AT THE SAME TIME evenly sk 3 (5, 0, 3, 1) sc, turn—7 (7, 9, 9, 11) ch-5 spaces.

Next row: Sk 1st sc, sl st in next 2 ch, ch 1, 2 sc in ch-space, *ch 3, 7-tr in next ch-space, ch 3**, 3 sc in next ch-space, rep from * across, ending last rep at **, 2 sc in last ch-space, turn—3 (3, 4, 4, 5) 7-tr groups, 6 (6, 8, 8, 10) ch-3 spaces and 2 (2, 3, 3, 4) 3-sc groups.

Last row: Ch 1, sc in 1st sc, *ch 7, (sc, ch 5, sc) in 4th tr of next tr group, ch 7, (sc, ch 5, sc) in 2nd sc of next sc group, rep from * across, fasten off.

PLAIN TOP

With B.

Rep Rows 28–31 and AT THE SAME TIME, work 2 sc in 3rd st of every 5th row, starting with Row 32, until you have 37 (38, 43, 49, 54) sts, then Rep Rows 28-31 without any increasing for a total of 67 (75, 79, 87, 95) rows in the leg.

Last row: Ch 4, sc in each st across, ch 4, sl st in the side of the last st, fasten off.

HEART APPLIQUE (MAKE 2)

With B.

Rnd 1: Ch 2, working in 2nd ch from hook (sc 2, hdc 2, dc, tr, ch 3, sl st, ch 3, tr, dc, hdc 2, sc 2, ch 3), sl st to 1st sc to join—12 sts (not including sl sts), 3 ch-3 spaces.

Rnd 2: Ch 1 (does not count as a st), sc 2, hdc 2, 3 dc in next st, 5 tr in next st, (dc, hdc, sc, sl st) in ch-3 space, (sl st, sc, hdc, dc) in next ch-3 space, 5 tr in next st, 3 dc in next st, hdc 2, sc 2, (sc, ch 3, sc) in ch-3 space, join—32 sts (not including sl sts), 1 ch-3 space.

Rnd 3: Ch 3 (counts as 1st dc), dc 6, 2 dc in each of next 5 sts, sc 3, sk next 2 sl sts, sc 3, 2 dc in each of next 5 sts, dc 8, (dc, ch 3, dc) in ch-3 space, dc in last, join—44 sts, 1 ch-3 space.

Fasten off B, change to C.

Rnd 4: Ch 1, hdc 7, 2 hdc in next 10 sts, hdc 6, 2 hdc in next 10 sts, hdc 9, 3 hdc in ch-3 space, hdc 2, join—67 hdc.

Rnd 5: Ch 1, working in BLO sc in each st around, join—67 sc.

Fasten off, leaving a long tail for sewing.

FINISHING

Fold one length of satin ribbon in half and pull through *bottom loop*. Pull ends through ribbon loop. Lace ribbon through *edge loops* as you would a corset and tie a bow at the top of the sock to hold in place.

Sew a Heart Applique to the outside half of the top of the sock, placing the bottom of the heart approximately 25 rows before the lace section. Weave in ends.

"I love making new friends and I respect people for a lot of different reasons."

–TAYLOR SWIFT

"You Belong with Me" Friendship Bracelet Pillow

Skill Level 1 2 3 4

Designed by Emily Davies

There's just something special about someone who really gets you. They know your favorite song, they know your favorite food, and they make you laugh harder than anyone else. Friendship with them is just easy and breezy!

Friendships come and go throughout our lives, but the real ones last forever. No matter how long it's been, you can send them a message or give them a call and it's like no time has passed at all. You can pick it right back up where you left it and just enjoy being together. Seeing each other in person is like a breath of fresh air and feels as natural as breathing.

One of the ways Taylor Swift fans have come to express friendship is by sharing and wearing friendship bracelets, especially if you're lucky enough to attend one of the concerts! We created the "You Belong with Me" Friendship Bracelet Pillow as a way to remember the happy times spent together and the many more to come. Crochet your pillow in your favorite colors, or make one for your bestie with theirs. And be sure to give it a good squishy hug to fill it with love.

Measurements

16" x 16" (40.5 x 40.5 cm)

Yarn

Worsted weight (#4 Medium)

Shown here: Lion Brand Color Theory, 246 yds (225 m), 3½ oz (100 g), 100% acrylic: 3 balls 122 Bone (A)

DK weight (#3 Light)

Shown here: Lion Brand Mandala Baby, 590 yds (539 m), 3½ oz (100 g), 100% acrylic: 1 ball 201 Rainbow Falls (B)

DK weight (#3 Light)

Shown here: Lion Brand 24/7 Cotton DK, 273 yds (249 m), 3½ oz (100 g), 100% cotton: 1 ball each 100 Sugarcane (C), 153 Caviar (D), and 149 Silver Lining (E)

Hooks

US H/8 (5 mm) crochet hook, US D/3 (3.25 mm) crochet hook. Adjust hook size if necessary to obtain correct gauge.

Notions

Yarn needle

Scissors

Locking stitch marker

Blocking supplies

16" x 16" (40.5 x 40.5 cm) pillow insert

Pom-pom maker (optional)

Gauge

15.5 hhdc x 12 rows = 4" (10 cm)

Notes

♥ Ch 1 at the beginning of a row does not count as a st.

♥ Pillow is worked in two flat panels that are seamed together.

♥ Bead appliques are made flat, and then stitched onto the chain, which is then all stitched onto the pillow.

CONTINUED

TAYLOR-MADE
FOR YOU

Customize the letters on your
friendship bracelet beads to
make something special and
specific to you!

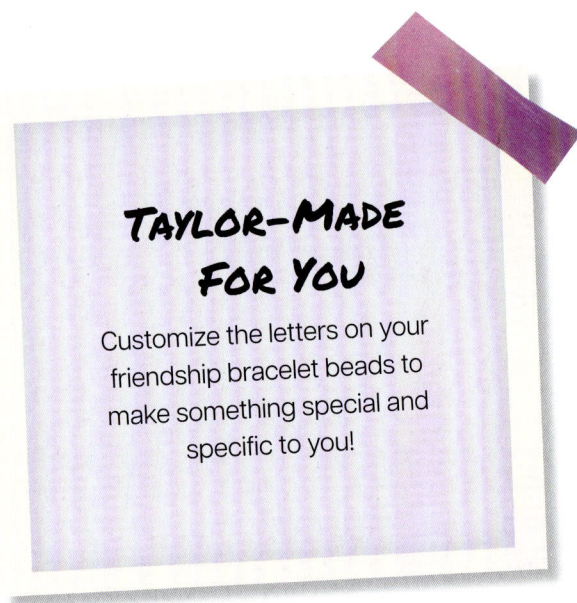

♥ Choose a light-colored pillow insert—white or beige
will work best.

♥ When working with the Mandala Baby, separate
it into individual sections based on colors—this will
ensure you can have a variety of colors!

♥ The circles for beads are worked in continuous
rounds—do not sl st to join unless indicated. Use
your stitch marker to mark the first st of each round
and move each subsequent round.

♥ Block your circles using the method of your choice.
Sample used steam blocking.

Special Stitches

Hhdc (Herringbone half double crochet): Yo, insert
hook into st and pull up a loop, pull 1st loop through the
2nd loop on hook, yo, pull through remaining two loops
on hook.

Magic Ring: Wrap yarn around two middle fingers from
back to front, insert crochet hook under loop, yo and
draw up a loop, yo and draw through loop (ch made).
Continue with 1st round crochet instructions. Pull loop
closed upon completion of 1st round crochet instructions. Secure end.

PILLOW PANELS (MAKE 2)

With larger hook and A.

Row 1 (WS): Ch 63, hhdc in 2nd ch from hook and in
each ch across, turn—62 hhdc.

Rows 2–48: Ch 1, hhdc across, turn—62 hhdc.

Fasten off.

SMALL CIRCLES (MAKE 13)

With smaller hook and B.

Rnd 1 (RS): Make a magic ring, sc 6 in ring, tighten
ring—6 sc.

Rnd 2: 2 sc in each st around—12 sc.

Rnd 3: *Sc 1, 2 sc in next, rep from * around—18 sc.

Rnd 4: *Sc 2, 2 sc in next, rep from * around—24 sc.

Rnd 5: *Sc 3, 2 sc in next, rep from * around—30 sc.

Rnd 6: *Sc 4, 2 sc in next, rep from * around—36 sc.

Rnd 7: *Sc 5, 2 sc in next, rep from * around—42 sc.

Rnd 8: Sc around, sl st to first st to join—42 sc.

Fasten off, leaving a long tail for sewing.

LARGE CIRCLES (MAKE 4)

With smaller hook and C.

Rnds 1-8: Rep Rnds 1-8 of Small Circles.

Rnd 9: *Sc 6, 2 sc in next, rep from * around, sl st to first
st to join—48 sc.

Fasten off, leaving a long tail for sewing.

BEAD EMBROIDERY

Working on Large Circles and using D and smaller hook,
surface sl st the letters Y, B, W, and M—one on each circle, using the photo as a guide. Alternatively, you could
embroider these on using your yarn needle.

BRACELET CHAIN

Using double strands of E and smaller hook, loosely ch 200. Before fastening off, check that your chain will drape across your pillow as desired. It should be at least 40" (101.5 cm) to completely drape around the pillow.

ASSEMBLY

Sew the WS of your circles to your bracelet chain using the long tail. The white circles should be in the middle of the chain, in the order of Y B W M. Leave about 0.5" (1.5 cm) between circles (to give room for sewing to the pillow).

Arrange your Pillow Panels so they are both RS facing out. Sl st through the edges of both panels up and around to join them. Once three sides are joined, slide in the pillow insert, then sl st the remaining side closed. Fasten off and weave in ends.

Arrange the bracelet on the pillow. Stitch the bracelet to it, sewing around the edge of each circle. It may be helpful to use locking stitch markers to hold the circles in place. For each circle, be sure to sew using the corresponding yarn color. The bracelet should wrap around the front and back of the pillow.

Once all circles are sewn to the pillow, use E to create mini "beads" between the circles. With a double strand of yarn and the yarn needle, wrap around the chain, down through the pillow panel, and back up on the other side of the chain. Continue wrapping yarn in this manner approximately 15 times between each circle.

Weave in all ends.

Optional: Using the pom-pom maker and remaining Mandala Baby yarn, create 4 pom-poms and attach one to each corner of the pillow.

"*No matter what happens in life, be good to people. Being good to people is a wonderful legacy to leave behind.*"

—TAYLOR SWIFT

"Karma" Cat Bag

Designed by Lee Sartori

What goes around comes around, so they say! Keeping that in the back of your mind during those tough days is especially important because it's not always easy to turn that frown upside down. Pressures from social media, work, school, friends, and family can all seem daunting and overwhelming, and the choices we make daily can affect so much. In "Karma," Taylor touches on how she built up resilience to negativity and how she finds the silver lining in every dark cloud. Karma is about the lessons learned from past mistakes or slights. It's about remembering that staying true to yourself and continuing to put one foot in front of the other can lead to amazing things. When things get scary, it helps to remember what makes you smile! Whether it's a treasured pet, a favorite color to wear, or a happy song that makes you want to dance around the kitchen, it's important to enjoy all the good things in life.

The "Karma" Cat Bag is a nod to some of those relaxing thoughts that Taylor sings about. The adorable cat on the front of the bag is sure to bring smiles wherever you go! The mint-colored background is a nod to the dress Taylor wears in the Karma music video; it really makes the cat image pop! The "Karma" Cat Bag is crocheted in what might be a new-to-you technique—the extended single crochet split stitch! This stitch mimics knit stitches and gives an amazingly clean color change. Finish off the bag with some fantastically sturdy Tunisian crocheted handles and you're ready to go shopping for your "just desserts"!

Measurements

22" (56 cm) wide x 17" (43 cm) tall, excluding handles

Yarn

DK weight (#3 Light)

Shown here: Lion Brand 24/7 Cotton DK, 273 yds (249 m), 3½ oz (100 g), 100% cotton: 6 balls 171 Fresh Mint (A), 1 ball 153 Caviar (B), 2 balls 100 Sugarcane (C)

DK weight (#3 Light)

Shown here: Lion Brand Coboo, 232 yds (212 m), 3½ oz (100 g), 51% cotton, 49% rayon from bamboo: 1 ball each 123 Tan (D), 125 Taupe (E), and 101 Pink (F)

Hook

US size B/1 (2.25 mm) crochet hook

Notions

Yarn needle

Stitch marker

Scissors

Gauge

Gauge is not critical for this project.

24 exsc x 28 rows = 4" (10 cm)

Notes

♥ This bag is worked in continuous rounds, changing yarn color following charts, creating the front and back panels at the same time. Each square of charts represents an extended single crochet stitch (exsc) worked in the indicated color.

♥ Once body of bag is worked, the bottom is seamed closed and handles are worked separately in Tunisian crochet and sewn to bag.

Special Stitches

FOR BAG

Exsc (extended single crochet): Insert hook into indicated st, yo and draw up a loop, yo and draw through 1 loop, yo and draw through 2 loops.

CONTINUED

TAYLOR-MADE FOR YOU

Change the colors of the cat on the bag to reflect a favorite pet of yours!

Exsc split st (extended single crochet split stitch): Insert hook between the posts of indicated stitch to "split the v" of the stitch, yo and draw up a loop, yo and draw through 1 loop, yo and draw through 2 loops.

FOR HANDLES

Basic Return: Ch 1, yo and draw through 2 loops on hook until end.

Tunisian Knit Stitch (tks): Insert hook from front to back through fabric and below chains formed by previous Return Round to right of front vertical thread but to left of corresponding back thread (between vertical posts), yo, draw loop through and leave on hook.

BAG

Rnd 1: With A, ch 260, join with a sl st in first ch to form a ring, taking care not to twist ch, ch 1, beg in same ch as joining sl st, exsc in first 130 ch, place a marker in last st made to indicate end of back of bag, exsc in next 130 ch, begin working in continuous rounds–260 exsc.

Place marker in last sc made to indicate end of rnd and end of front of bag. Move markers up as each rnd is completed.

The remainder of the bag is worked in exsc split st. The first 130 sts are allotted for the back of the bag, and the last 130 sts are allotted for the front of the bag (the colorwork section).

Rnd 2: With A, exsc split st to first marker for back of bag; exsc split st to end of rnd AND change yarn color following Row 2 of chart for front of bag

Rnd 3–120: With A, exsc split st to first marker; exsc split st to end of rnd AND change yarn color following next row of chart.

Fasten off, weave in ends.

SEAMING

Because of the nature of crochet stitches, they tend to 'lean' to the left a minute amount over each row. You can block your bag at this point to straighten out the image a bit. To account for the "lean," the bag was crocheted in continuous rounds to avoid visible side seams. To section out the front and back panels for seaming, center the image of the cat over equal parts of the front and back of the bag and mark each of the bottom edges with a stitch marker. Turn the bag inside out and using A, seam the bottom of the bag closed between the two marked edges. Weave in ends and turn bag right-side out.

HANDLES (MAKE 2)

With A, leave a long tail for sewing at start of Row 1.

Row 1: Ch 10, starting in the 2nd ch from the hook draw up a loop in every ch across (10 loops on hook), do not turn, complete Basic Return.

Rows 2–140: Tks across, complete Basic Return.

Fasten off, leaving a long tail for sewing.

FINISHING

With bag laying flat and RS facing, mark handle placement with a stitch marker approximately 5" (12.5 cm) in from the side edges, and approximately 8 rounds from the top of the bag. Sew one handle to the front and one handle to the back of the bag. Weave in ends.

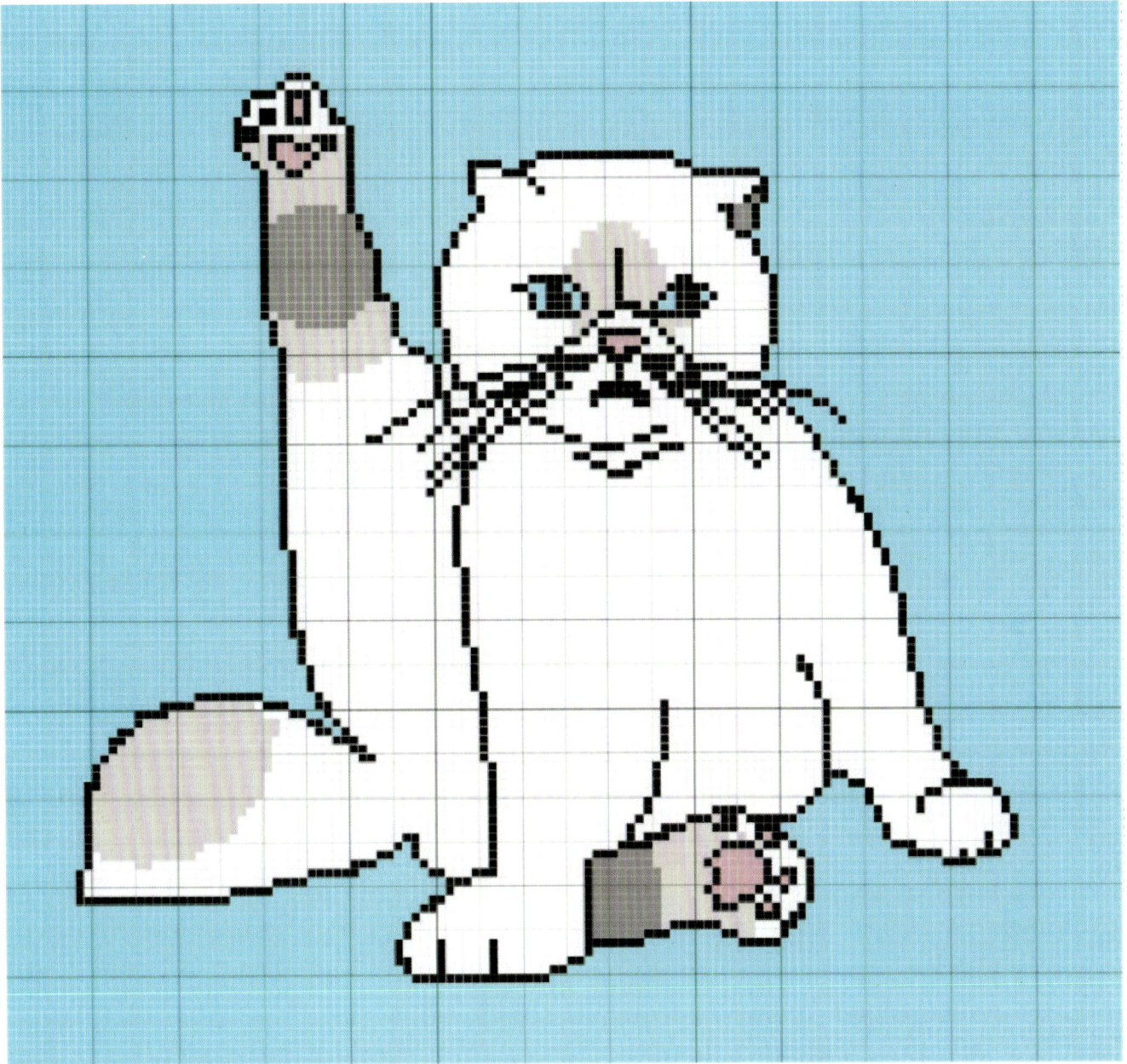

KEY

- ▨ Fresh Mint (A)
- ■ Caviar (B)
- □ Sugarcane (C)
- ▨ Tan (D)
- ▨ Taupe (E)
- ▨ Pink (F)

Scan to access complete color charts for this project.

CHAPTER Four

BLOSSOM

"Anytime someone tells me that I can't do something, I want to do it more."

—TAYLOR SWIFT

Growing and learning are part of everything, even crochet! We all had to start somewhere in our crochet journey, whether it was making our first hat or our first blanket. Practice makes perfect, and doing is learning when it comes to crocheting our favorite things. I'm so happy that you are taking a journey with the projects in this book! For the last chapter, I hope you enjoy whimsical projects like the "Wildest Dreams" Cardigan, and the "Bejeweled" Headband. I can't wait to see your beautiful makes!

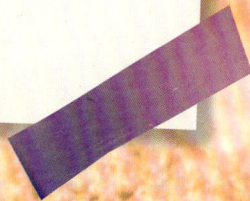

"My style advice to other girls is to be experimental but always have a 'home base' and stick with your comfort style."

—TAYLOR SWIFT

"Style" Newsboy Cap

Skill Level

1 2 3 4

Designed by Lee Sartori

Certain styles can withstand the test of time, rising above trends and becoming endearing classics—like the allure of a classic red lip, or the charm of a fantastic newsboy cap! We all have those stand-out pieces in our wardrobe that we go to over and over again because they go with absolutely everything.

Imagine crocheting something so awesome—like one of those timeless classics in your closet—that friends and family members asked you to make one for them, too. When you know how to crochet, it's inevitable that friends will ask you to whip up something special for them. We've all been there. Luckily this is a fast and gorgeous project to work on and you'll be stitching up gifts for all your besties in no time!

This newsboy crochet pattern is worked from the top down, meaning you'll be starting at the crown and stitching "round and round" to create the body of the hat. Finish by adding a structured brim, a final touch that elevates your creation from a mere accessory to a fashion statement that you'll return to again and again.

Size

S (M, L)

Measurements

Head circumference: 21 (22, 23)" [53.5 (56, 58.5) cm]

Yarn

Worsted weight (#4 Medium)

Shown here: Lion Brand Re-Spun Bonus Bundle (please note that this yarn is listed as a 4-weight but works up as a lightweight 2/3), 658 yds (601 m), 10 oz (284 g), 100% recycled polyester: 1 ball 186 Amber

Hook

US size C/2 (2.5 mm) crochet hook. Adjust hook size if necessary to obtain correct gauge.

Notions

Yarn needle

Plastic mesh

Stitch marker

Scissors

Gauge

Work measures 1" (2.5 cm) across after Round 4, and 4" (10 cm) after Round 16.

25 sc worked in the round = 4" (10 cm)

Notes

♥ Hat is worked from the crown downwards, with a brim worked separately and sewn on.

♥ Using anything but the recommended yarn can significantly change the gauge—please match gauge for intended fit.

Special Stitch

inv-dec (invisible single crochet decrease): Insert hook in front loop only of each of next 2 sts, yarn over and draw through both sts, yarn over and draw through 2 loops on hook—1 st decreased.

CONTINUED

CAP

Rnd 1: Ch 2, 6 sc in 2nd ch from hook—6 sc.

Place marker in last sc made to indicate end of rnd. Move marker up as each rnd is completed.

Rnd 2: 2 sc in each st around—12 sc.

Rnd 3: [2 sc, sc in next st] around—18 sc.

Rnd 4: [Sc, 2 sc in next st, sc] around—24 sc.

Rnd 5: [2 sc, sc 3] around—30 sc.

Rnd 6: [Sc 2, 2 sc in next st, sc 2] around—36 sc.

Rnd 7: [2 sc, sc 5] around—42 sc.

Rnd 8: [Sc 3, 2 sc in next st, sc 3] around—48 sc.

Rnd 9: [2 sc, sc 7] around—54 sc.

Rnd 10: [Sc 4, 2 sc in next st, sc 4] around—60 sc.

Rnd 11: [2 sc, sc 9] around—66 sc.

Rnd 12: [Sc 5, 2 sc in next st, sc 5] around—72 sc.

Rnd 13: [2 sc, sc 11] around—78 sc.

Rnd 14: [Sc 6, 2 sc in next st, sc 6] around—84 sc.

Rnd 15: [2 sc, sc 13] around—90 sc.

Rnd 16: [Sc 7, 2 sc in next st, sc 7] around—96 sc.

Rnd 17: [2 sc, sc 15] around—102 sc.

Rnd 18: [Sc 8, 2 sc in next st, sc 8] around—108 sc.

Rnd 19: [2 sc, sc 17] around—114 sc.

Rnd 20: [Sc 9, 2 sc in next st, sc 9] around—120 sc.

Rnd 21: [2 sc, sc 19] around—126 sc.

Rnd 22: [Sc 10, 2 sc in next st, sc 10] around—132.

Rnd 23: [2 sc, sc 21] around—138 sc.

Rnd 24: [Sc 11, 2 sc in next st, sc 11] around—144 sc.

Rnd 25: [2 sc, sc 23] around—150 sc.

Rnd 26: [Sc 12, 2 sc in next st, sc 12] around—156 sc.

Rnd 27: [2 sc, sc 25] around—162 sc.

Rnd 28: [Sc 13, 2 sc in next st, sc 13] around—168 sc.

Rnd 29: [2 sc, sc 27] around—174 sc.

Rnd 30: [Sc 14, 2 sc in next st, sc 14] around—180 sc.

Rnd 31: [2 sc, sc 29] around—186 sc.

Rnd 32: [Sc 15, 2 sc in next st, sc 15] around—192 sc.

Rnd 33: [2 sc, sc 31] around—198 sc.

Rnd 34: [Sc 16, 2 sc in next st, sc 16] around—204 sc.

Rnd 35: [2 sc, sc 33] around—210 sc.

Rnd 36: [Sc 17, 2 sc in next st, sc 17] around—216 sc.

*sl st in the next st.

Rnd 37: Ch 1, working in BLO, sc around, do not join—216 sc.

Rnds 38–44: Sc around.

Rnd 45: [Sc 17, inv-dec, sc 17] around—210 sc.

Rnd 46: [Inv-dec, sc 33] around—204 sc.

Rnd 47: [Sc 16, inv-dec, sc 16] around—198 sc.

Rnd 48: [Inv-dec, sc 31] around—192 sc.

*sl st in next st.

Rnd 49: Ch 1, working in BLO [sc 15, inv-dec, sc 15] around, do not join—186 sc.

Rnd 50: [Inv-dec, sc 29] around—180 sc.

Rnd 51: [Sc 14, inv-dec, sc 14] around—174 sc.

Rnd 52: [Inv-dec, sc 27] around—168 sc.

Rnd 53: [Sc 13, inv-dec, sc 13] around—162 sc.

Rnd 54: [Inv-dec, sc 25] around—156 sc.

Rnd 55: [Sc 12, inv-dec, sc 12] around—150 sc.

Rnd 56: [Inv-dec, sc 23] around—144 sc.

Size L Only: Proceed to Lengthening Round.

Rnd 57: [Sc 11, inv-dec, sc 11] around—138 sc.

Size M Only: Proceed to Lengthening Round.

Rnd 58: [Inv-dec, sc 21] around—132 sc.

Size S Only: Proceed to Lengthening Round.

Lengthening Round: Sc around.

Fasten off, weave in ends.

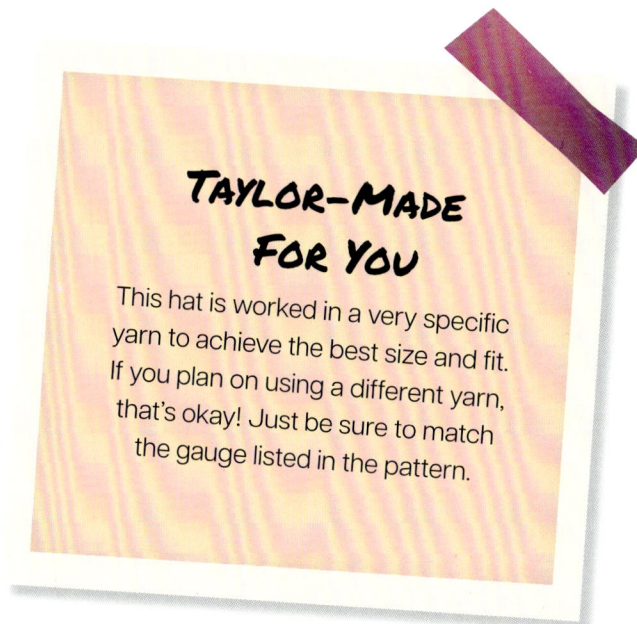

TAYLOR-MADE FOR YOU

This hat is worked in a very specific yarn to achieve the best size and fit. If you plan on using a different yarn, that's okay! Just be sure to match the gauge listed in the pattern.

BRIM (MAKE 2)

Row 1: Ch 2, 2 sc in 2nd ch from hook, turn—2 sc.

Row 2: Ch 1, sc, 2 sc in last st, turn—3 sc.

Row 3: Ch 1, 2 sc, sc across, turn—4 sc.

Rows 4–18: Rep Rows 2–3—19 sc at end of Row 18.

Rnd 19: Rep Row 3—20 sc.

Rows 20–99: Ch 1, sc across, turn.

Row 100: Ch 1, sc across to last 2 sts, sc2tog, turn—19 sc.

Row 101: Ch 1, sc2tog, sc across, turn—18 sc.

Rows 102–117: Rep Rows 100–101—2 sc remaining.

Fasten off.

MESH INSERT

Lace a piece of the brim over your plastic mesh and trace the shape with a marker. Cut out the piece to insert into the brim after joining.

JOINING

With two pieces atop each other, sc around front of brim through both thicknesses, leaving the straight/long edge open. Turn piece right-side out to hide joining seam inside, insert plastic mesh. Sew remaining edge closed.

FINISHING

Sew Brim to front of hat across the long/straight edge. Weave in ends.

"Wildest Dreams" Cardigan

Designed by Wilma Westenberg

One of the most exciting things you can do in life is to finally take a chance on something that you have been dreaming about. It's especially exciting when you get to share it with someone you love! I was lucky enough to have one of those experiences recently when my family and I decided to move across Canada to live in a place close to the ocean. It was a big move and we left behind all of our family and friends. While it was a bit stressful and at times we felt a little homesick, we have spent our time making memories and experiencing a brand new life. Our dreams included sandy beaches, seeing whales, and spending time hiking along the sea. It was absolutely wonderful to turn that dream into a reality!

"Wildest Dreams" is an homage to taking those chances and living your best life. It captures those dreamy moments and those sparkling memories that make life worth living. Nothing lasts forever and it's important to live the way you want to live.

The "Wildest Dreams" Cardigan is a sparkly, glitzy number perfect for a night out doing something that makes you happy! This design is inspired by the 1989 World Tour and the glittery outfits Taylor Swift wore while playing at her bedazzled piano. With easy construction and simple stitches, this cardigan is the perfect crochet project for a beginner crocheter!

Size

XS (S, M, L, XL, 2XL, 3X, 4X, 5X)

Measurements

To fit bust: 28–30 (32–34, 36–38, 40–42, 44–46, 48–50, 52–54, 56–58, 60–62) [71–76 (81.5–86.5, 91.5–96.5, 101.5–106.5, 112–117, 122–127, 132–137, 142–147.5, 152.5–157.5) cm]

Actual bust: 32 (36, 40, 44, 48, 52, 56, 60, 64)" [81.5 (91.5, 101.5, 112, 122, 132, 142, 152.5, 162.5) cm]

Length: 20 (20, 20, 20, 20.5, 20.5, 20.5, 21, 21)" [51 (51, 51, 51, 52, 52, 52, 53.5, 53.5) cm]

Yarn

Worsted weight (#4 Medium)

Shown here: Lion Brand North Pole Yarn Co. Sparkle Yarn, 164 yds (150 m), 3½ oz (100 g), 56% acrylic, 44% polyester: 6 (7, 8, 8, 9, 10, 11, 11, 12) balls 150 Silver

Hook

US size J/10 (6 mm) crochet hook. Adjust hook size if necessary to obtain correct gauge.

Notions

Yarn needle

Scissors

Measuring tape

Zipper (15" [40 cm])

Needle and thread or a sewing machine for adding a zipper

Gauge

12 sts x 11 rows in whdc = 4" (10 cm)

Notes

♥ Pattern is worked from back panel bottom-up to first front panel without breaking yarn, and rejoined for second front panel. Sleeves are worked independently and seamed to armhole. Sleeves and sides are seamed and zipper is added last.

CONTINUED

- ♥ Cardigan is designed with a 2–4" (5–10 cm) positive ease.
- ♥ Cardigan is shown in size S.
- ♥ Turning chains do not count as a stitch.
- ♥ Crochet loosely to make working with sequins easier.

Special Stitches

Bpdc (back post double crochet): Yarn over, insert the hook from back to front to back around the post of the stitch, yarn over and pull up a loop, then (yarn over and pull through 2 loops) twice.

Fpdc (front post double crochet): Yarn over, insert the hook from front to back to front around the post of the stitch, yarn over and pull up a loop, then (yarn over and pull through 2 loops) twice.

Whdc (wide half double crochet): Half double crochet worked in between the stitches

Fdc (foundation double crochet): Ch 2, yarn over, insert hook into first ch, pull up a loop, yarn over, pull through one loop, yarn over, pull through two loops, yarn over, pull through two loops.

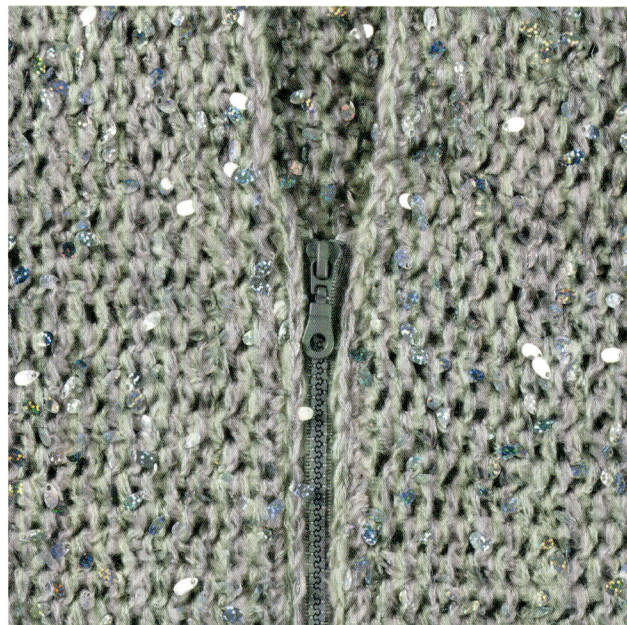

TAYLOR-MADE FOR YOU

The "Wildest Dreams" Cardigan features the addition of a zipper, but you can omit it for a different look!

BACK PANEL

Row 1: 46 (52, 58, 64, 70, 76, 82, 86, 92) Fdc, turn.

Row 2: Ch 3, *fpdc, bpdc; rep from * across, turn.

Rep Row 2 until piece measures 2" (5 cm) from beg.

Next row: Ch 2, whdc in each st across, turn—46 (52, 58, 64, 70, 76, 82, 86, 92) sts.

Rep last row until piece measures 20 (20, 20, 20, 20.5, 20.5, 20.5, 21, 21)" [51 (51, 51, 51, 52, 52, 52, 53, 53) cm] from beg.

Do not fasten off.

FRONT PANELS

Row 1: Ch 2, whdc in next 23 (26, 29, 32, 35, 38, 41, 43, 46) sts, turn; leave rem sts unworked for second front panel.

Row 2: Ch 2, whdc in each st across, turn.

Rep Row 2 until front panel measures 18 (18, 18, 18, 18.5, 18.5, 18.5, 19, 19)" [46 (46, 46, 46, 47, 47, 47, 48, 48) cm] from beg.

Next 4 rows: Ch 3, *fpdc, bpdc; rep from * across, turn.

Fasten off and leave a long tail for seaming the sides later.

Reattach the yarn in the stitch after the first front panel and rep these steps for the second front panel.

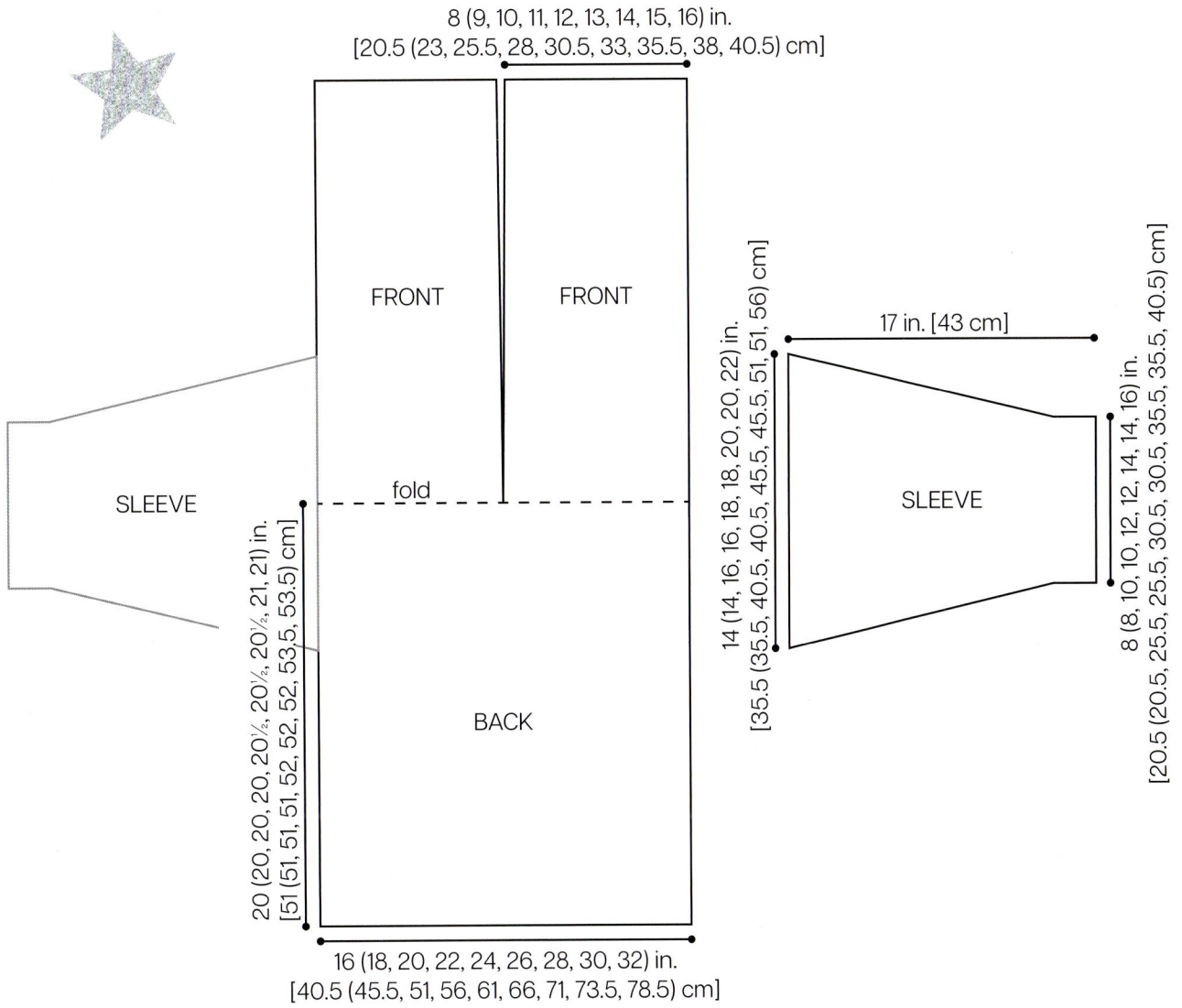

8 (9, 10, 11, 12, 13, 14, 15, 16) in.
[20.5 (23, 25.5, 28, 30.5, 33, 35.5, 38, 40.5) cm]

FRONT

FRONT

SLEEVE

fold

20 (20, 20, 20, 20½, 20½, 21, 21) in.
[51 (51, 51, 52, 52, 52, 53.5, 53.5) cm]

BACK

16 (18, 20, 22, 24, 26, 28, 30, 32) in.
[40.5 (45.5, 51, 56, 61, 66, 71, 73.5, 78.5) cm]

17 in. [43 cm]

SLEEVE

14 (14, 16, 16, 18, 20, 20, 22) in.
[35.5 (35.5, 40.5, 40.5, 45.5, 51, 51, 56) cm]

8 (8, 10, 10, 12, 12, 14, 14, 16) in.
[20.5 (20.5, 25.5, 25.5, 30.5, 30.5, 35.5, 35.5, 40.5) cm]

> *"If you are lucky enough to find something that you love, and you have a shot at being good at it, don't stop, don't put it down."*
>
> **–TAYLOR SWIFT**

SLEEVES (MAKE 2)

Row 1: 26 (26, 32, 32, 38, 38, 44, 44, 50) Fdc, turn.

Row 2: Ch 3, *fpdc, bpdc; rep from * across, turn.

Rep Row 2 until piece measures 2" (5 cm) from beg. Width should measure 8 (8, 10, 10, 12, 12, 14, 14, 16)" [20.5 (20.5, 25.5, 25.5, 30.5, 30.5, 35.5, 35.5, 40.5) cm].

Row 5: Ch 2, 1 hdc in each st across, turn.

Row 6: Ch 2, 2 whdc in first st, 1 hdc in each st across, 2 hdc in last st, turn—28 (28, 34, 34, 40, 40, 46, 46, 52) sts.

Rows 7–9: Ch 2, whdc in each st across, turn.

Rep Rows 6–9 until a total of 33 rows have been worked—40 (40, 46, 46, 52, 52, 58, 58, 64) sts.

Rows 34–44: Ch 2, whdc in each st across, turn.

The sleeve width should now measure 14 (14, 16, 16, 18, 18, 20, 20, 22)" [35.5 (35.5, 40.5, 45.5, 45.5, 45.5, 51, 51, 56) cm], and the total sleeve length should be 17" (43 cm).

Fasten off, leaving a long tail end for sewing the sleeve to the body. Rep these steps for the second sleeve.

ASSEMBLY

Decide which side will be the RS based on your preferences. Lay the body panel and sleeves out flat with the RS facing up. Align the center stitches of the last row of the sleeve with the shoulder point of the front panel (where the back panel ends and the front begins) and sew the sleeves to the body using a yarn needle. Fold the front panels on top of the back panel with the RS facing outward. Fold the sleeves lengthwise and sew the sleeves and side seams. Sewing tip: Use scissors to remove the sequins to make sewing easier.

ZIPPER

With RS facing, attach yarn so that you are ready to work up a front edge, sc across row ends up one front edge and down the next front edge. Fasten off, weave in ends. Use needle and thread or a sewing machine for the zipper. Zipper sewing tip: You may want to pin the zipper in place about every 2" (5 cm) to stabilize it before sewing.

"Your feelings so are important to write down, to capture, and to remember because today you're heartbroken, but tomorrow you'll be in love again."

—TAYLOR SWIFT

"Blank Space" Journal Cover

Skill Level 1 2 3 4

Designed by April Rongero

One of the best parts about continuing to grow in life is the realization that it's up to us to be the people we want to be. It's not about what other people are saying about us, or what other people are thinking about us. It's about how we feel about ourselves, and the actions we take on a daily basis. We can't control the opinions of others, but we can control the voice inside our own heads. In "Blank Space" Taylor Swift takes control of the narrative that she is a serial dater and that loving her will only end in heartache. She takes all of the bricks that were thrown at her and builds a beautiful garden for herself. She's grown as a person and understands what it is to be in the driver's seat of her own life.

The " Blank Space " Journal Cover is a nod to taking that ownership and facing it with a wink and a smile! It features four sweet little hearts on the front cover of the journal, and a stunning houndstooth stitch cover on the back. Fill this journal with your plans, hopes, and dreams! Or maybe just a list of your favorite crochet patterns—that would be amazing, too!

Size

Designed to fit a standard 1" (2.5 cm) 3-ring binder

Measurements

Front and back flaps: 10½" (26.5 cm) wide x 11.625" (29.5 cm) high

Spine: 1.375" (3.5 cm) wide x 11.625" (29.5 cm) high

Finished cover size: 22" (56 cm) wide x 11½" (29 cm) high, when measured flat

Yarn

DK weight (#3 Light)

Shown here: Lion Brand Yarns Coboo, 232 yds (212 m), 3½ oz (100 g), 51% cotton, 49% rayon from bamboo: 1 ball each 147 Plume (A), 102 Pale Pink (B), 123 Tan (C), 152 Coal (D), 099 Vanilla Blossom (E)

Hook

US size G/6 (4 mm) crochet hook. Adjust hook size if necessary to obtain correct gauge.

Notions

Yarn needle

Stitch markers

Scissors

Gauge

18 sts x 15 rows in lemon peel st = 4" (10 cm)

Notes

- This notebook cover is worked in one piece. Four appliqué hearts are then sewn on the front panel.

- The front and back halves are worked using intarsia crochet, which uses separate balls of yarn for each section of color.

- The pockets are worked in joined and turned rounds. The center portion is worked in rows.

- The ch 1 at the beginning of rounds and rows does not count as a stitch. The sl st used to join rounds does not count as a stitch unless noted.

- Stitch markers are optional, but you may find them helpful for marking the first st of a round or row.

Special Stitches

Lemon peel stitch (sc, dc): Alternating sc and dc. When each row or round is worked, sc is always worked into dc, and dc is always worked into sc.

CONTINUED

Magic Ring: Wrap yarn around two middle fingers from back to front, insert crochet hook under loop, yo and draw up a loop, yo and draw through loop (ch made). Continue with 1st round crochet instructions. Pull loop closed upon completion of 1st round crochet instructions. Secure end.

TAYLOR-MADE FOR YOU

This journal would make a great scrapbook for your Eras Tour memorabilia!

BACK POCKET

Rnd 1 (RS): With A, ch 51, sc in back bump of 2nd ch from hook and in each ch across, rotate to work along opposite side of foundation ch; change to B, sc 25 in the opposite side of foundation ch; change to C, sc 25 across, sl st to 1st st, turn—100 sts.

Rnd 2: With C, ch 1, [sc, dc] x 12, sc; change to B, dc, [sc, dc] x 12; change to A, [sc, dc] across, sl st to 1st st, turn.

Rnd 3: With A, ch 1, [sc, dc] x 25; change to B, [sc, dc] x 12, sc; change to C, dc, [sc, dc] x 12, sl st to 1st st, turn.

Rnds 4–19: Rep Rnds 2–3.

Rnd 20: With C, ch 1, [sc, dc] x 12, sc; change to B, dc, [sc, dc] x 12; change to A, sc across, sl st to 1st st, turn.

Rnd 21: With A, ch 1, sc 50, 2 sc in next st, dc, [sc, dc] x 11, sc; change to D, dc, [sc, dc] x 11, sc, (dc, sc) in last st, sl st to 1st st, turn—102 sts.

Fasten off C and B. Continue to Back Half.

BACK HALF

Row 1 (WS): With D, ch 1, hdc, [sc, dc] x 12, sc; change to A, dc, [sc, dc] x 12, hdc in next st; leave remaining sts unworked, turn—52 sts.

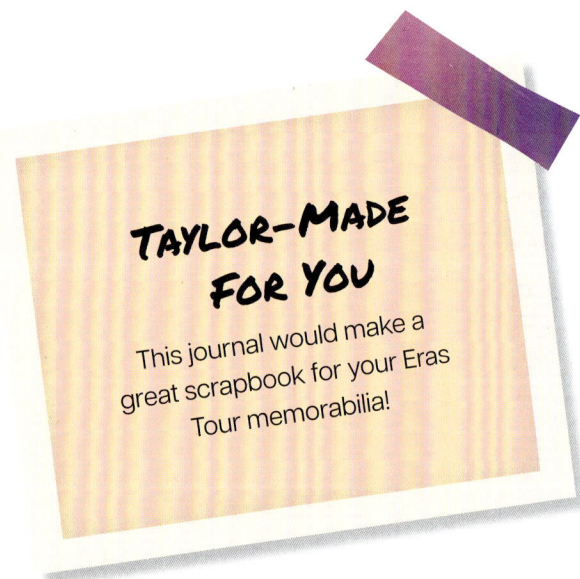

Row 2: With A, ch 1, hdc, [sc, dc] x 12, sc; change to D, dc, [sc, dc] x 12, hdc in last st, turn.

Rows 3–19: Rep Rows 1–2.

Fasten off D and A. Change to E and continue to Spine.

SPINE

Row 1 (RS): Ch 1, hdc, [sc, dc] across to last st, hdc, turn—52 sts.

Rows 2–7: Rep Row 1.

Fasten off E and change to A. Continue to Front Half.

FRONT HALF

Row 1 (WS): Ch 1, hdc, [sc, dc] x 12, sc; change to C, dc, [sc, dc] x 12, hdc in last st, turn—52 sts.

Row 2: With C, ch 1, hdc, [sc, dc] x 12, sc; change to A, dc, [sc, dc] x 12, hdc in last st, turn.

Rows 3–18: Rep Rows 1–2.

Row 19/Rnd 1 (WS): With A, ch 1, hdc, [sc, dc] x 12, sc; change to C, dc, [sc, dc] x 12, hdc in last st, ch 50, sl st to 1st, turn—102 sts.

Continue to Front Pocket.

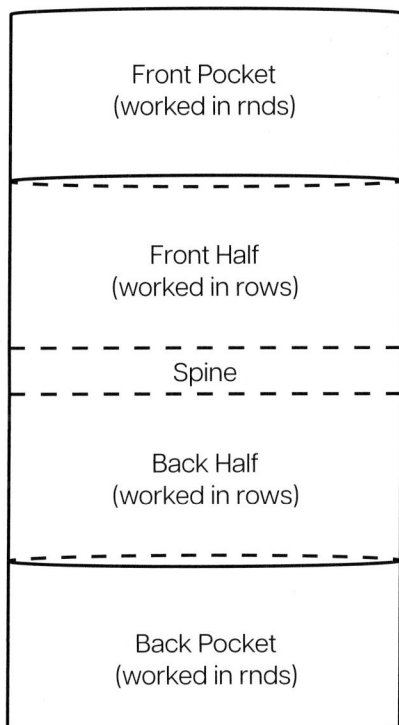

```
┌─────────────────────────────┐
│                             │
│   Front Pocket              │
│   (worked in rnds)          │
│                             │
├─────────────────────────────┤
│                             │
│   Front Half                │
│   (worked in rows)          │
│                             │
├ ─ ─ ─ ─ ─ ─ ─ ─ ─ ─ ─ ─ ─ ─ ┤
│   Spine                     │
├ ─ ─ ─ ─ ─ ─ ─ ─ ─ ─ ─ ─ ─ ─ ┤
│                             │
│   Back Half                 │
│   (worked in rows)          │
│                             │
├─────────────────────────────┤
│                             │
│   Back Pocket               │
│   (worked in rnds)          │
│                             │
└─────────────────────────────┘
```

FRONT POCKET

Rnd 2 (RS): With C, ch 1, sc 50; change to D, sc2tog, dc, [sc, dc] x 11, sc; change to B, dc, [sc, dc] x 11, sc, dc2tog, sl st to 1st st, turn—100 sts.

Rnd 3: With B, ch 1, [sc, dc] x 12, sc; change to D, dc, [sc, dc] x 12; change to C, [sc, dc] across, sl st to 1st st, turn.

Rnd 4: With C, ch 1, [sc, dc] x 25; change to D, [sc, dc] x 12, sc; change to B, dc, [sc, dc] x 12, turn.

Rnds 5–19: Rep Rnds 3–4. After last rep, fasten off D and B. Flip pocket inside out.

Rnd 20: With C, ch 1, turn, insert hook through both layers and sc across to close the pocket—50 sts.

Fasten off.

HEART APPLIQUÉ (MAKE 3 OF D AND 1 OF E)

Rnd 1 (RS): In magic ring, ch 2 (does not count as a st), dc 12, sl st to 1st st, do not turn—12 sts.

Rnd 2: Ch 2, 2 dc in next 4 sts, 2 hdc in next st, (hdc, sc) in next st, (sc, hdc) in next st, 2 hdc in next st, 2 dc in next 4 sts, sl st to 1st st—24 sts.

Rnd 3: Ch 1, do not turn, sc in same st, (hdc, dc) in next st, dc, 2 dc in next st, dc, 2 hdc in next st, [sc, 2 sc in next st] x 2, hdc, (dc, tr) in next st, (tr, dc) in next st, hdc, [2 sc in next st, sc] x 2, 2 hdc in next st, dc, 2 dc in next st, dc, (dc, hdc) in next st, sc, do not sl st—36 sts.

Rnd 4: Ch 1, turn, sc in same st, hdc, (hdc, dc) in next st, dc 2, 2 dc in next st, (dc, hdc) in next st, hdc, sc 9, (sc, hdc) in next st, (hdc, sc) in next st, sc 9, hdc, (hdc, dc) in next st, 2 dc in next st, dc 2, (dc, hdc) in next st, hdc, sc, sl st into Rnd 3 between halves, sl st to 1st st of round—46 sts, including sl sts.

Fasten off, leaving a long tail for sewing.

FINISHING

Using photographs as a guide, sew all hearts to the front panel. The three D hearts should be sewn in the center of the B, A, and C squares. The E heart should be sewn in the center of the D square. Weave in any remaining ends.

Reputation *Taylor Doll*

Skill Level 1 **2** 3 4

Designed by Lee Sartori

There are *so* many amazing and iconic outfits worn by Taylor Swift. Not only from her music videos, but from her tours as well! It can be hard to choose, but I decided to go with one that hadn't yet been referenced with any of the other projects. For the second version of the Taylor Doll, I went with the amazing bodysuit that Taylor wears for her *Reputation* Tour. It's a jet-black suit with cut-outs for the arm and leg, and it's adorned with several swirly red snakes that wind around the body.

The Reputation Tour was a way for Taylor to gain back some of her storylines and grow as a person. She used everything that had been thrown at her and turned it into an incredible album of ownership and empowerment. I hope that stitching away on this doll gives you a moment to reflect on how amazing you are and how far you have come! It's important to look back, but it's even more important to look forward and keep taking steps towards the person we want to be. We have the opportunity to learn and grow every single day, to own our mistakes, and to make better decisions. And what doesn't make us happy like a great crochet project, right?

Measurements

14" (35.5 cm) tall

Yarn

Worsted weight (#4 Medium)

Shown here: Lion Brand Basic Stitch Anti-Pilling, 185 yds (169 m), 3½ oz (100 g), 100% acrylic: 1 ball each 121 Almond (A), 153 Black (B), 158 Mustard (C)

DK weight (#3 Light)

Shown here: Lion Brand 24/7 Cotton DK, 273 yds (249 m), 3½ oz (100 g), 100% cotton: 1 ball 113 Grenadine (D)

Hooks

US size D/3 (3.25 mm) crochet hook, US size B/1 (2.25 mm) crochet hook. Adjust hook size if necessary to obtain correct gauge.

Notions

Fiberfill

1 pair 12 mm black or blue safety eyes

Black embroidery thread

White embroidery thread

Yarn needle

Stitch marker

Scissors

Gauge

Gauge is not critical for this project.

24 sc x 26 rows = 4" (10 cm)

Note

♥ The doll is worked bottom up, with arms made separately and added in as the body progresses.

Special Stitches

Fsc (foundation single crochet): Ch 2, insert hook in 2nd ch from hook and pull up loop, yo and pull through 1 loop (ch made), yo and pull through 2 loops (sc made), *insert hook in ch of previous st and pull up loop, yo and pull through 1 loop (ch made), yo and pull through 2 loops (sc made); repeat from * for required number of fsc.

Hdc2tog (half double crochet 2 together): Yo and insert hook in indicated st, yo and draw up a loop, yo and insert hook into next st, yo draw up a loop, yo and draw through all loops on hook.

Hdc3tog (half double crochet 3 together): Yo and insert hook in indicated st, yo and draw up a loop, [yo and insert hook into next st, yo and draw up a loop] twice, yo and draw through all loops on hook.

inv-dec (invisible single crochet decrease): Insert hook in front loop only of each of next 2 sts, yarn over and draw through both sts, yarn over and draw through 2 loops on hook—1 st decreased.

CONTINUED

TAYLOR-MADE FOR YOU

Add a bit of glittery thread to your snakes to really make them pop!

LEFT ARM

With A, and larger hook.

Rnd 1: Ch 5, beg in 2nd ch from hook, sc 3, 3 sc in next ch, rotate to work on the underside of ch, sc 3, 3 sc in last ch—12 sc.

Place marker in last sc made to indicate end of rnd. Move marker up as each rnd is completed.

Rnd 2: Sc 4, 2 sc in next st, sc 5, 2 sc in next st, sc in last st—14 sc.

Rnd 3: Sc around.

Rnd 4: Sc 6, ch 3, 3 sc in 2nd ch from hook (thumb made), sc in next ch, sc 8—18 sc.

Rnd 5: Sc 6, sk 4 sc of thumb, sc 8—14 sc.

Rnd 6: [Sc 5, inv-dec] twice—12 sc.

Stuff hand; continue stuffing arm as work progresses.

Rnd 7: [Sc 4, inv-dec] twice—10 sc.

Change to B.

Rnds 8–22: Sc around.

Fasten off, set aside to join to Body at indicated rnd.

RIGHT ARM

Make same as Left Arm, working Rnds 1-4 with A, and Rnds 8-22 with B.

SHOES (MAKE 2)

With B, and larger hook.

Rnd 1: Ch 9, sc in 2nd ch from hook, sc 6, 3 sc in next ch, rotate to work on the underside of ch, sc 7, 3 sc in last ch—20 sc.

Place marker in last sc made to indicate end of rnd. Move marker up as each rnd is completed.

Rnd 2: Sc 7, 2 sc in each of next 3 sts, sc 8, 3 sc in next st, sc in last st—25 sc.

Rnd 3: Sc 7, [2 sc, sc in next] x 3, sc 9, 3 sc in next, sc in last 2—30 sc.

Fasten off 1st piece. Repeat Rnd 1–3 for 2nd piece, but do not fasten off.

Rnd 4: With 2 pieces atop one another and working through both thicknesses, sc around—30 sc.

Rnd 5: Sc 7, [sc, inv-dec] x 3, sc 14—27 sc.

Rnd 6: Sc 7, inv-dec, hdc2tog x 2, inv-dec, sc 12—23 sts.

Rnd 7: Sc, Inv-dec x 3, hdc3tog x 2, inv-dec x 3, sc 2, inv-dec—12 sts.

Fasten off; stuff the shoe. Do not overstuff. Continue to Legs.

LEFT LEG

With B, and larger hook, join to back of heel.

Rnds 1–4: Ch 1, sc around, join with a sl st to 1st st—12 sc.

Rnd 5: Ch 1, sc around, join with a sl st to 1st st.

Rnd 6a (Boot Cuff): Ch 1, working in FLO, [2 hdc, hdc in next st] around, sl st to join—18 hdc. Fasten off.

Rnd 6b: Rejoin A to BLO of st in back of heel of Rnd 5, ch 1, sc 11, 2 sc in last, join—13 sc.

Rnd 7: Ch 1, sc 12, 2 sc in last st, join—14 sc.

Rnd 8: Ch 1, sc 13, 2 sc in last st, join—15 sc.

Rnds 9–10: Ch 1, sc around, join—15 sc.

Rnd 11: Sc around, do not join.

Rnd 12: Sc 3, [sc, 2 sc in next st] x 4, sc 4—19 sc.

Rnd 13: Sc 5, inv-dec, [2 sc, sc in next] x 3, 2 sc in next st, inv-dec, sc 3—21 sc.

Rnd 14: Sc 6, inv-dec x 6, sc 3—15 sc.

Rnd 15: [Sc 4, 2 sc in next st] around—18 sc.

Rnd 16: [Sc 5, 2 sc in next st] around—21 sc.

Rnd 17: [Sc 6, 2 sc in next st] around—24 sc.

Rnds 18–25: Sc around.

Fasten off. Stuff leg.

RIGHT LEG

Make same as left leg, working all rnds with B. Stuff leg. Continue to Body.

BODY

With B, and larger hook.

With back of Legs facing, mark st in middle of each inner thigh where legs will join.

Rnd 1: With back of Legs facing and beginning in marked st, sc 24 around 1st leg, ch 3, sc in marked st of 2nd leg, sc around—48 sc, ch-3.

Place marker in last sc made to indicate end of rnd. Move marker up as each rnd is completed.

Rnd 2: Sc in each of next 3 ch, sc 24, sc in underside of next 3 ch, sc 24—54 sc.

Rnd 3: 2 sc in next st, 3 sc in next st, 2 sc in next 2 sts, sc around to last st, 2 sc in last st—60 sc.

Rnds 4–12: Sc around.

Rnd 13: Sc 4, sc3tog, sc 4, sc3tog, sc around to last 3 sts, sc3tog—54 sc.

Rnds 14–16: Sc around.

Rnds 17–23: Sc around.

Incorporate arms into next round.

Rnd 24: With B, sc 19; with A, sc 10 around Left Arm, ensuring that thumb is facing body; continuing with B, sc 27, sc 10 around Right Arm, ensuring that thumb is facing body, sc 8—74 sc.

Rnd 25: With B, sc 19; with A, sc 4, inv-dec, sc 4; with B, sc 31, inv-dec, sc 12—72 sc.

Rnd 26: With B, [sc 5, inv-dec, sc 10, inv-dec]; with A, sc 9; with B, sc, inv-dec, sc 5, [sc 5, inv-dec, sc 5] x 3—66 sc.

Rnd 27: With B, sc 9, inv-dec, sc 6; with A, sc 3, inv-dec, sc 4; with B, sc 5, inv-dec, [sc 9, inv-dec] x 3—60 sc.

Stuff arms and body; continue stuffing as work progresses.

Rnd 28: With B, sc 4, inv-dec, sc 8, inv-dec; with A, sc 8; with B, inv-dec, sc 4, [sc 4, inv-dec, sc 4] x 3—54 sc.

Rnd 29: With B, sc 7, inv-dec, sc 5; with A, sc 2, inv-dec, sc 4; with B, sc 3, inv-dec, [sc 7, inv-dec] x 3—48 sc.

Rnd 30: With B, sc 3, inv-dec, sc 6, inv-dec; with A, sc 6, inv-dec; with B, [sc 6, inv-dec] x 3, sc 3—42 sc.

Rnd 31: With B, sc 5, inv-dec, sc 4; with A, sc, inv-dec, sc 4; with B, sc, inv-dec, [sc 5, inv-dec] x 3—36 sc.

Rnd 32: With B, sc 2, inv-dec, sc 4, inv-dec; with A, sc 4, inv-dec; with B, sc 4, inv-dec, sc 2, [sc 2, inv-dec, sc 2] x 3—30 sc.

Rnd 33: With B, sc 3, inv-dec, sc 3; with A, inv-dec, sc 3; with B, inv-dec, [sc 3, inv-dec] x 3– 24 sc.

Fasten off A, continue with B.

Rnd 34: [Sc, inv-dec, sc] around—18 sc.

Rnd 35: Sc around.

Finish stuffing, paying close attention to stuffing tops of arms/shoulders firmly.

Fasten off B, change to A. Continue to Head.

HEAD

With A, and larger hook.

Rnd 1: Working in BLO, sc around—18 sc.

Place marker in last sc made to indicate end of rnd. Move marker up as each rnd is completed.

Rnd 2: 2 sc in each st around—36 sc.

Rnd 3: [Sc 5, 2 sc in next st] around—42 sc.

Rnd 4: [Sc 3, 2 sc in next st, sc 3] around—48 sc.

Rnd 5: [Sc 7, 2 sc in next st] around—54 sc.

Rnd 6: [Sc 4, 2 sc in next st, sc 4] around—60 sc.

Rnd 7: [Sc 9, 2 sc in next st] around—66 sc.

Rnds 8–21: Sc around.

Insert eyes in between Rnds 15 and 16, 12 sts apart. Before adding the safety backing, use white embroidery thread to add white detail to lower lid of eye, and black embroidery thread to add eyelashes. Using A, add nose detail between Rnds 12 and 13 over 3 sts. Using a length of A, cinch the eyes together by sewing a line between both eyes and pulling the line taut to create a slight dent.

Rnd 22: [Sc 9, inv-dec] around—60 sc.

Rnd 23: [Sc 4, inv-dec, sc 4] around—54 sc.

Rnd 24: [Sc 7, inv-dec] around—48 sc.

Rnd 25: [Sc 3, inv-dec, sc 3] around—42 sc.

Stuff Head and continue stuffing as work progresses.

Rnd 26: [Sc 5, inv-dec] around—36 sc.

Rnd 27: [Sc 2, inv-dec, sc 2] around—30 sc.

Rnd 28: [Sc, 3, inv-dec] around—24 sc.

Rnd 29: [Sc, inv-dec, sc] around—18 sc.

Rnd 30: [Sc, inv-dec] around—12 sc.

Rnd 31: Inv-dec around—6 sc.

Fasten off, leaving a long tail for sewing; sew remaining 6 sts closed. Weave in ends.

HAIR CROWN

With C and larger hook, work in BLO for entire piece.

Rnd 1: Ch 2, 6 sc in 2nd ch from hook—6 sc.

Place marker in last sc made to indicate end of rnd. Move marker up as each rnd is completed.

Rnd 2: 2 sc in each st around—12 sc.

Rnd 3: [2 sc, sc in next] around—18 sc.

Rnd 4: [Sc, 2 sc in next, sc in next] around—24 sc.

Rnd 5: [2 sc, sc in next 3] around—30 sc.

Rnd 6: [Sc 2, 2 sc in next, sc 2] around—36 sc.

Rnd 7: [2 sc, sc in next 5] around—42 sc.

Rnd 8: [Sc 3, 2 sc in next, sc 3] around—48 sc.

Rnd 9: [2 sc, sc in next 7] around—54 sc.

Rnd 10: [Sc 4, 2 sc in next, sc 4] around—60 sc.

Rnd 11: [2 sc, sc in next 9] around—66 sc.

Rnds 12–14: Sc around. Begin working in turned rows.

Row 15: In BLO, sc 48, turn, leaving remaining 18 sts unworked—48 sc.

Row 16: Ch 1, sk 1st st, working in FLO across, sc 45, inv-dec, turn—45 sc.

Row 17: Ch 1, sk 1st st, working in BLO across, sc 42, inv-dec, turn—43 sc.

Row 18: Ch 1, sk 1st st, working in FLO across, sc 40, inv-dec, turn—41 sc.

Fasten off, leaving a long tail for sewing. Sew Hair Crown to top of head with 18 sts of Row 15 set at forehead, 7 rnds above edge of safety eyes. Weave in ends.

HAIR

The hair for this doll is worked in 2 parts. The bangs are made first, then the long hair around the entire circumference of the Hair Crown.

Bangs

With C and larger hook. Hold doll facing away from you. Using two stitch markers, mark out the skipped 18 stitches across the center of the forehead of Rnd 15 of Hair Crown.

Row 1: Working in FLO, sl st to 1st marked st, [ch 6, sc in 2nd ch from hook and in next 4 ch, sl st in next 2 sts of Rnd 15 of Hair Crown] 8 times, ch 6, sc in 2nd ch from hook and in next 4 ch, sl st in next st—9 bang strands.

Fasten off, weave in ends. Secure center 5 strands of bangs to forehead by tacking them down using C. Leave 2 strands on each edge untacked/unsewn.

Long Hair

With C and larger hook.

Rnd 1: Sl st to 1st FLO st of Rnd 1 of Hair Crown, [ch 41, hdc in 2nd ch from hook, hdc in next 39 ch, sl st in next 3 sts of Hair Crown] working through each FLO st of Rnd 1.

Rnd 2: Repeat as per Rnd 1 around FLO sts of Rnd 2 of Hair Crown.

Continuing Rnds: Sk 3 rounds of Hair Crown by working sl sts in FLO to Rnd 6 of Hair Crown. Repeat Rnd 1 around Rnd 6. Sk next 3 rounds to Rnd 10 of Hair Crown and repeat Rnd 1 around Rnd 10. Continue skipping 3 rounds of Hair Crown and completing a new round of hair until piece ends.

Fasten off, weave in ends. Starting with final rounds of hair, begin tacking down hair strands to head to smooth hair. Hair strands can overlap each other.

SNAKES (MAKE 4)

With smaller hook and D.

Row 1: Leaving a long beg tail for sewing, ch 2, sc in 2nd ch from hook, turn—1 sc.

Row 2: Ch 1, 4 sc in sc, turn—4 sc.

Row 3: Ch 1, [sc2tog] x 2, turn—2 sc.

Row 4: Ch 1, sc2tog, do not turn—1 sc.

Row 5: Ch 2, beg in 2nd ch from hook, fsc 100—100 sc.

Fasten off, leaving a long tail for sewing.

FINISHING

Using photos as a guide, secure the 4 snakes to the right side (the black side) of the body suit. One of the snakes will coil around the arm. One of the snakes will wrap around the neck and create the first arch for the chest. The next snake will begin below the opposite side of the chest and create the arch, wrapping behind the back. The final snake begins mid-chest and swirls down the right leg. Weave in ends.

"I'd like to think you don't stop being creative once you get happy."

—TAYLOR SWIFT

"Bejeweled" Headband

Skill Level: 1 2 3 4

Designed by Rachel Misner

It can be tough when we feel underappreciated. Whether you are a student studying day and night to get a good grade, a friend who remembers birthdays, or a hard worker at a job that seems thankless, it can all take a toll on your self-confidence. "Bejeweled" is about making sure you know that despite what you may be thinking, you are a jewel, a valuable spark, and an absolute gem, no matter what. Taylor Swift is a pro at finding her inner strength and reclaiming her confidence as a person and as an artist, and in "Bejeweled" she shares that with her listeners. She makes sure that no one takes her for granted, and continues to sparkle and shine. It's a song about encouragement and knowing your value. Keep your head up and shine like a diamond!

The "Bejeweled" Headband is a beautiful wearable based on the necklace Taylor wears in the "Bejeweled" music video. Made with variegated yarn and bobble stitches to mimic beautiful jewels, this project is fun and beginner friendly. Finish the headband off by sewing some glittery gems along the outside edges for that extra sparkle!

Size

Child (Tween, Adult)

Measurements

Finished circumference: 15.75 (16.5, 17.25)" [40 (42, 44.5) cm]

Finished width: 3 (3, 3)" [7.5 (7.5, 7.5) cm], at widest point

Yarn

DK weight (#3 Light)

Shown here: Lion Brand Superwash Merino, 306 yds (279 m), 3½ oz (100 g), 100% merino wool: 1 ball 098 Antique (A)

DK weight (#3 Light)

Shown here: Lion Brand Mandala Sequins, 295 yds (269 m), 3½ oz (100 g), 98% acrylic, 2% polyester: 1 ball 200 Tanzanite (B)

Hook

US size G/6 (4.00 mm) crochet hook. Adjust hook size if necessary to obtain correct gauge.

Notions

Yarn needle

Scissors

20 (22, 24) sew-on crystals (13 x 3 mm)

Sewing needle and thread

Gauge

11 sts x 11 rows in Sc BLO = 2" (5 cm)

Notes

♥ This headband is worked in rows, then seamed together to join.

♥ This is a very stretchy headband. The finished measurements will stretch several inches to fit the head. You can adjust the fit even further by adding or removing Rows 1–4 of the Even Section as many times as needed.

♥ Work all bobbles with B. To change yarn color, work last stitch of previous color to last yarn over. Yarn over with new color and draw through all loops on hook to complete stitch. Proceed with new color. When changing to B, do not cut A. Crochet the bobble over the A-colored strand to avoid floats and to keep yarn hidden. When changing to A, cut B and leave a tail to weave in later.

♥ Unwind and separate B into individual balls of color. Pick 6 or more different colors. Use a different color for each bobble and rotate evenly throughout as you go. You can pick colors at random or keep them in order. Sample has colors picked at random.

Special Stitches

Bobble (Bo): *Yo, insert hook into indicated st, yo and pull up a loop, yo and pull through 2 loops on hook; rep from * 2 more times, yo pull through all 4 loops on hook.

CONTINUED

Increase Section

With A.

Row 1 (RS): Ch 6, sc in 2nd ch from hook and in each ch across, turn—5 sc.

Row 2: Ch 1, sc in 1st st, sc BLO in each st to last st, sc in last st, turn.

Rows 3–7: Rep Row 2.

Row 8: Ch 1, 2 sc in 1st st, sc BLO in each st to last st, 2 sc in last st, turn—7 sc.

Rows 9–20: Rep Rows 3–8 twice—11 sc in Row 20.

Rows 21–25: Rep Row 2.

Row 26: Ch 1, sc in 1st st, sc 4 BLO, Bo BLO, sc 4 BLO, sc in last st, turn—10 sc, 1 Bo.

Row 27: Rep Row 2—11 sc.

Row 28: Rep Row 8—13 sc.

Row 29: Rep Row 2.

Row 30: Ch 1, sc in 1st st, sc 3 BLO, Bo BLO, sc 3 BLO, Bo BLO, sc 3 BLO, sc in last st, turn—11 sc, 2 Bo.

Rows 31–33: Rep Row 2—13 sc.

Row 34: Ch 1, 2 sc in 1st, sc BLO, Bo BLO, [sc 3 BLO, Bo BLO] x 2, sc BLO, 2 sc in last st, turn—12 sc, 3 Bo.

Even Section

Rows 1–3: Ch 1, sc in 1st st, sc BLO in each st to last st, sc in last st, turn—15 sc.

Row 4: Ch 1, sc in 1st st, sc 2 BLO, Bo BLO, [sc 3 BLO, Bo BLO] x 2, sc 2 BLO, sc in last st, turn—12 sc, 3 Bo.

Rows 3–16 (20, 24): Rep Rows 1–4 for 3 (4, 5) more times.

Decrease Section

Row 1: Ch 1, sc2tog, sc BLO in each st to last 2 sts, sc2tog, turn—13 sc.

Rows 2–3: Ch 1, sc in 1st st, sc BLO in each st to last st, sc in last st, turn.

Row 4: Ch 1, sc in 1st st, sc 3 BLO, Bo BLO, sc 3 BLO, Bo BLO, sc 3 BLO, sc in last st, turn—11 sc, 2 BO.

Rows 5–6: Rep Row 2.

Row 7: Rep Row 1—11 sc.

Row 8: Ch 1, sc in 1st st, sc 4 BLO, Bo BLO, sc 4 BLO, sc in last st, turn—10 sc, 1 Bo.

Rows 9–14: Rep Row 2—11 sc.

Row 15: Rep Row 1—9 sc.

Row 16–20: Rep Row 2.

Rows 21–26: Rep Rows 15–20—7 sc.

Row 27: Rep Row 1—5 sc.

Rows 28–33: Rep Row 2.

Fold your headband in half with RS together. Working on WS, join the first and last rows together by slip stitching across, working through both thicknesses to join. Flip headband RS out. Do not fasten off.

Trim

Rnd 1: Ch 1, sc into the end of each row around opening of headband, sl st to 1st sc to join—87 (91, 95) sc.

Fasten off.

Join yarn with a sl st to 1st row next to the seam on the other side of the headband.

Rnd 1: Ch 1, sc into the end of each row, sl st to 1st sc to join—87 (91, 95) sc.

Fasten off.

Finishing

Sew the crystals to the headband.

Weave in all ends.

TAYLOR-MADE FOR YOU

Change up the colors of the yarn to mimic your favorite jewels for this headband!

"I think fearless is having fears but jumping anyway"

–TAYLOR SWIFT

"Fearless" Fingerless Gloves

Skill Level 1 2 **3** 4

Designed by Lee Sartori

It's funny how one person can make you feel on top of the world, as if you could do absolutely anything. The possibilities are endless because you draw all of the strength and confidence you need to get anything done. And not only that, but that person has a special way of making even the most mundane things like driving around seem so special and fun. They take away all your anxieties and stress and make you smile. It's so lovely! The "Fearless" Gloves aim to capture that feeling, with a nod to the same confidence and strength.

There are so many great ways to add color work to crochet and it seems like everyone has a favorite. One of mine is the magic of the "extended single crochet split stitch." It might sound like a mouthful, but trust me, the results are nothing short of fantastic. This technique creates clean, faux-knit stitches that can elevate your crochet projects to a whole new level of awesomeness! This stitch is a game-changer, and once you give it a shot, you'll be crafting gloves that scream "Fearless" on one hand and "Flawless" on the other. Imagine keeping these stylish gloves for yourself or gifting them to someone special—a friend you'd love to dance in the rain or jump in puddles with!

Size

Small (Medium, Large)

Measurements

Circumference around hand: 6⅓ (7, 7¾)" [16 (18, 19.5) cm]

Yarn

Worsted weight (#4 Medium)

Shown here: Lion Brand Basic Stitch Anti-Pilling, 185 yds (169 m), 3½ oz (100 g), 100% acrylic: 2 balls 106 Baby Blue (A), 1 ball 099 Ivory (B)

Hook

US size E/4 (3.5 mm) crochet hook. Adjust hook size if necessary to obtain correct gauge.

Notions

Yarn needle

Scissors

Gauge

20 sc x 24 rows in BLO = 4" (10 cm)

Notes

♥ Follow chart for color work section.

♥ Color chart is worked right side facing only. Fasten off at the end of each row and reattach in 1st stitch of row without turning to start a new row.

Special Stitches

Bphdc (back post half double crochet): Yo and insert hook around post of next st from back to front, pushing the post backward, yo and draw up a loop, yo and draw through 3 loops.

Exsc (extended single crochet): Insert hook into indicated st, yo and draw up a loop, yo and draw through 1 loop, yo and draw through 2 loops.

Exsc split st (extended single crochet split stitch): Insert hook between the 'v' or posts of indicated st, yo and draw up a loop, yo and draw through 1 loop, yo and draw through 2 loops.

Fphdc (front post half double crochet): Yo and insert hook around post of next st from front to back pushing the post forward, yo and draw up a loop, yo and draw through 3 loops.

CONTINUED

TAYLOR-MADE FOR YOU

Fingerless gloves are perfect for a bit of warmth and coziness, while still freeing up your fingers for texting and taking photos. But for those extra chilly days, add a pair of mittens under these gloves for an extra layer of warmth!

RIGHT GLOVE "FEARLESS"

With A.

Row 1 (RS): Ch 46, sc in 2nd ch from hook and in each ch across, turn—45 sc.

Rows 2–3: Ch 1, working in BLO sc across, turn.

Row 4: Ch 1, working in BLO exsc across, fasten off.

Rows 5–13: Ch 1, working each st in color indicated in chart, exsc split st across, fasten off.

Note: Work in BLO for remainder of pattern.

Row 14: Ch 1, sl st in 1st 5 sl sts, sc 10, sl st 15, sc 15, turn.

Row 15: Ch 1, sc 15, sl st 15, sc 10, sl st 5, turn—45 sts.

Rows 16–38 (42, 46): Rep Rows 14–15, ending with a Row 14.

Fasten off.

Joining Row: With RS facing, join final round to underside of starting chain by stitching through both thicknesses. The top of the glove is the end with the 5 sl sts. The bottom is the end with the 15 sc. The word "Fearless" will start at the top and end at the bottom. Join to bottom edge, ch 1, sc 30 through both thicknesses, sc in next 10 sts of underside of starting ch only, skip 10 sts of last row worked (thumb hole made), sc through both thicknesses of last 5 sts. Thumb hole should be near the beginning of the word "Fearless." Fasten off.

Proceed to Cuff instructions.

LEFT GLOVE "FLAWLESS"

With A.

Rows 1–4: Rep Rows 1–4 of Right Glove.

Rows 5–13: Rep Rows 5–13 of Right Glove, following "Flawless" Color chart.

Row 14: Ch 1, sc 15, sl st 15, sc 10, sl st 5, turn—45 sts.

Row 15: Ch 1, sl st in first 5 sl sts, sc 10, sl st 15, sc 15, turn.

Rows 16–38 (42, 46): Rep Rows 14–38 (42, 46) of Right Glove.

Fasten off.

Joining Row: With RS facing, join final round to underside of starting chain by stitching through both thicknesses. The top of the glove is the end with 5 sl sts. The bottom is the edge with 15 sc. The word "Flawless" will start at the bottom and end at the top. Join to the bottom edge, ch 1, sc 5 through both thicknesses, sc in next 10 sts of underside of starting ch only, skip 10 sts of last row worked (thumb hole made), sc through both thicknesses of last 30 sts. Thumb hole should be near the end of the word "Flawless." Fasten off.

Proceed to Cuff instructions.

CUFF

With A.

With RS facing, join to any row end of bottom edge of glove.

Rnd 1: Ch 1, sc 40 (44, 48) evenly around bottom edge of glove; join with sl st in 1st sc—40 (44, 48) sc.

Rnd 2: Ch 1, hdc in each st around, join with sl st in first hdc.

Rnds 3–4: Ch 1, [2 fphdc, 2 bphdc] around, join with sl st in first st—40 (44, 48) sts.

Fasten off, weave in ends.

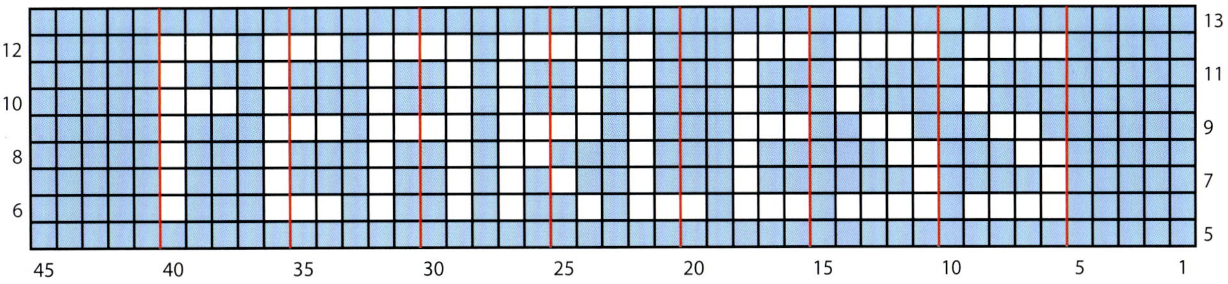

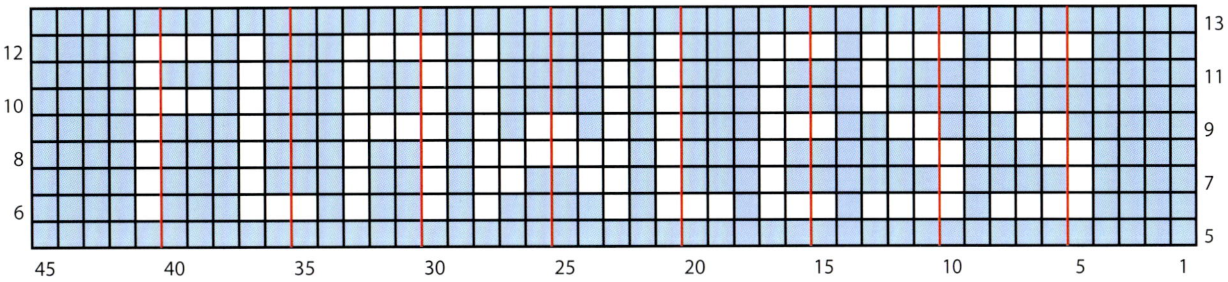

Key

- = Baby Blue (A)
- = Ivory (B)

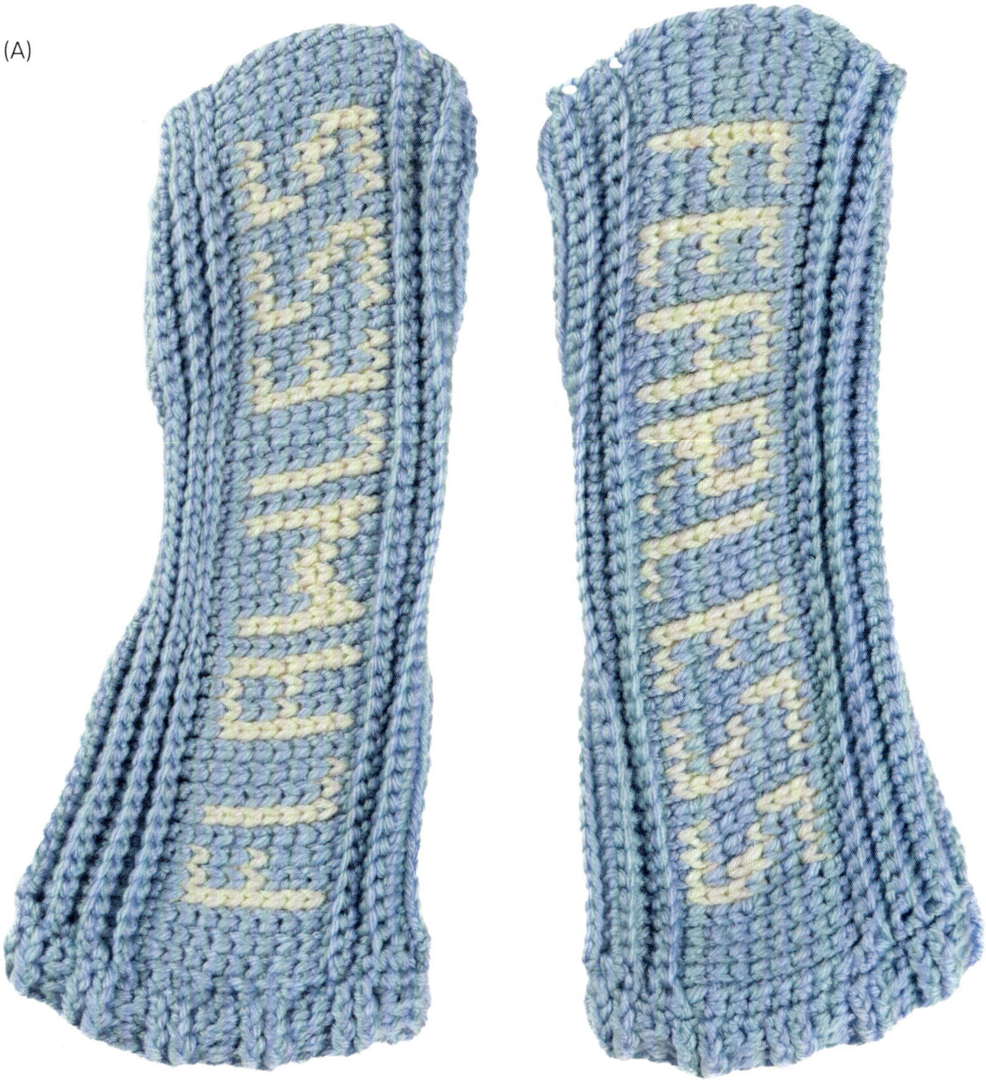

CROCHET STITCHES AND TECHNIQUES

If you're new to crochet, use these pages to learn the basic techniques and most common stitches. If you're a seasoned stitcher, you may still want to refer to this section to brush up on techniques or learn new ones.

Basic Skills

Slip Knot and Chain

All crochet begins with a chain, into which is worked the foundation row for your piece. To make a chain, start with a slip knot. To make a slip knot, make a loop several inches from the end of the yarn, insert the hook through the loop, and catch the tail with the end (1). Draw the yarn through the loop on the hook (2). After the slip knot, start your chain. Wrap the yarn over the hook (yarn over) and catch it with the hook. Draw the yarn through the loop on the hook. You have now made 1 chain. Repeat the process to make a row of chains. When counting chains, do not count the slip knot at the beginning or the loop that is on the hook (3).

Slip Stitch

The slip stitch is a very short stitch, which is mainly used to join 2 pieces of crochet together when working in rounds. To make a slip stitch, insert the hook into the specified stitch, wrap the yarn over the hook (1), and then draw the yarn through the stitch and the loop already on the hook (2).

Single Crochet

Insert the hook into the specified stitch, wrap the yarn over the hook, and draw the yarn through the stitch so there are 2 loops on the hook (1). Wrap the yarn over the hook again and draw the yarn through both loops (2). When working in single crochet, always insert the hook through both top loops of the next stitch, unless the directions specify front loop or back loop only.

Half Double Crochet

Wrap the yarn over the hook, insert the hook into the specified stitch, and wrap the yarn over the hook again (1). Draw the yarn through the stitch so there are 3 loops on the hook. Wrap the yarn over the hook and draw it through all 3 loops at once (2).

Double Crochet

Wrap the yarn over the hook, insert the hook into the specified stitch, and wrap the yarn over the hook again. Draw the yarn through the stitch so there are 3 loops on the hook (1). Wrap the yarn over the hook again and draw it through 2 of the loops so there are now 2 loops on the hook (2). Wrap the yarn over the hook again and draw it through the last 2 loops (3).

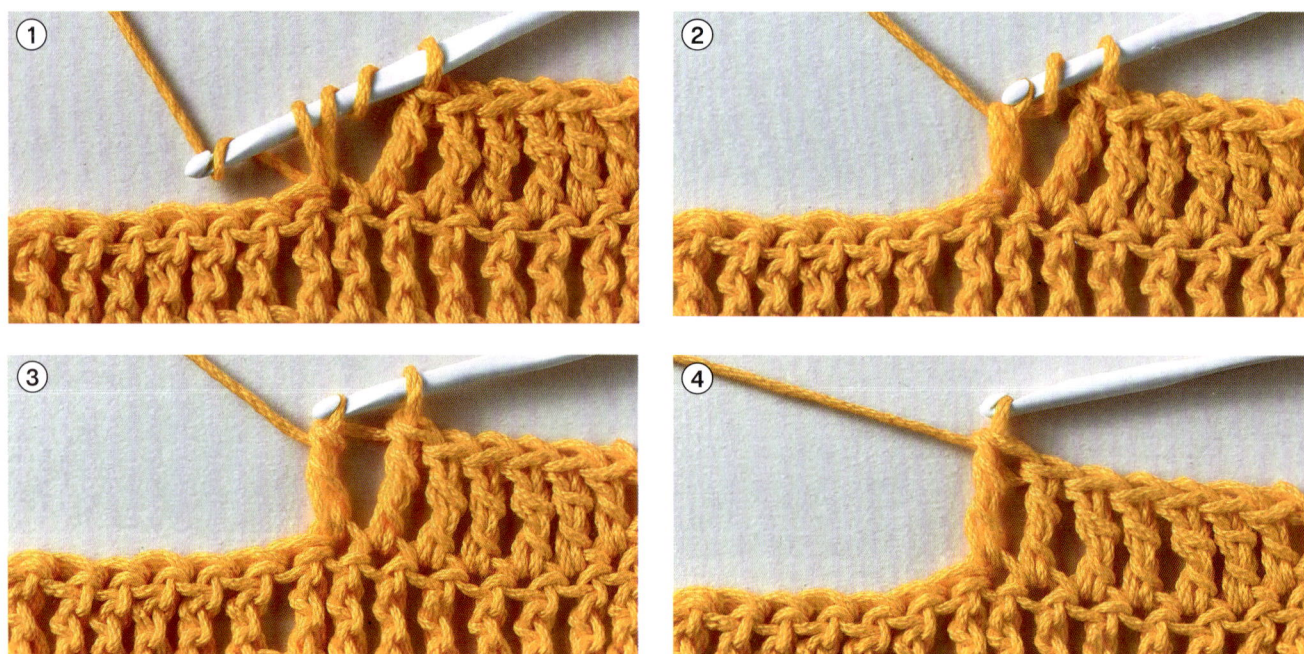

Treble Crochet

Wrap the yarn over the hook twice, insert the hook into the specified stitch, and wrap the yarn over the hook again. Draw the yarn through the stitch so there are 4 loops on the hook. Wrap the yarn over the hook again (1) and draw it through 2 of the loops so there are now 3 loops on the hook (2). Wrap the yarn over the hook again and draw it through 2 of the loops so there are now 2 loops on the hook (3). Wrap the yarn over the hook again and draw it through the last 2 loops (4).

Working Through the Back Loop

This creates a distinct ridge on the side facing you. Insert the hook through the back loop only of each stitch, rather than under both loops of the stitch. Complete the stitch as usual.

INCREASING AND DECREASING

To shape your work, you will often increase or decrease stitches as directed by the pattern. To increase in a row or round, you crochet twice into the same stitch, thereby increasing the stitch count by 1. To increase at the end of a row, you chain extra stitches, then turn and work into those stitches, thereby increasing the stitch count.

To decrease in a row or round, you crochet 2 (or more) stitches together as directed, thereby decreasing the stitch count. The technique varies depending on which crochet stitch you are using.

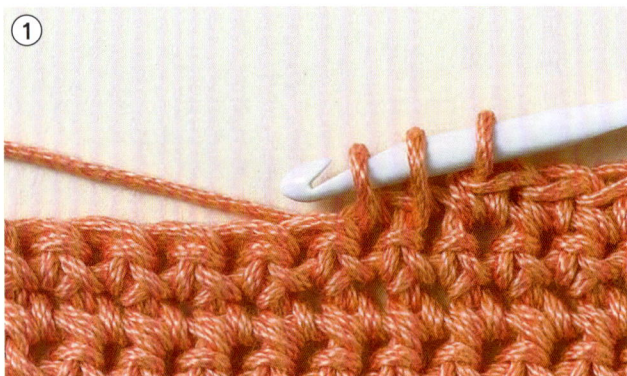

Single Crochet Two Stitches Together

This decreases the number of stitches in a row or round by 1. Insert the hook into the specified stitch, wrap the yarn over the hook, and draw the yarn through the stitch so there are 2 loops on the hook (1). Insert the hook through the next stitch, wrap the yarn over the hook, and draw the yarn through the stitch so there are 3 loops on the hook (2). Wrap the yarn over the hook again and draw the yarn through all the loops at once.

Double Crochet Two Stitches Together

This decreases the number of stitches in a row or round by 1. Wrap the yarn over the hook, insert the hook into the specified stitch, and wrap the yarn over the hook again. Draw the yarn through the stitch so there are 3 loops on the hook. Wrap the yarn over the hook again and draw it through 2 of the loops so there are now 2 loops on the hook. Wrap the yarn over the hook and pick up a loop in the next stitch, so there are now 4 loops on the hook. Wrap the yarn over the hook and draw through 2 loops. Wrap yarn over and draw through 3 loops to complete the stitch.

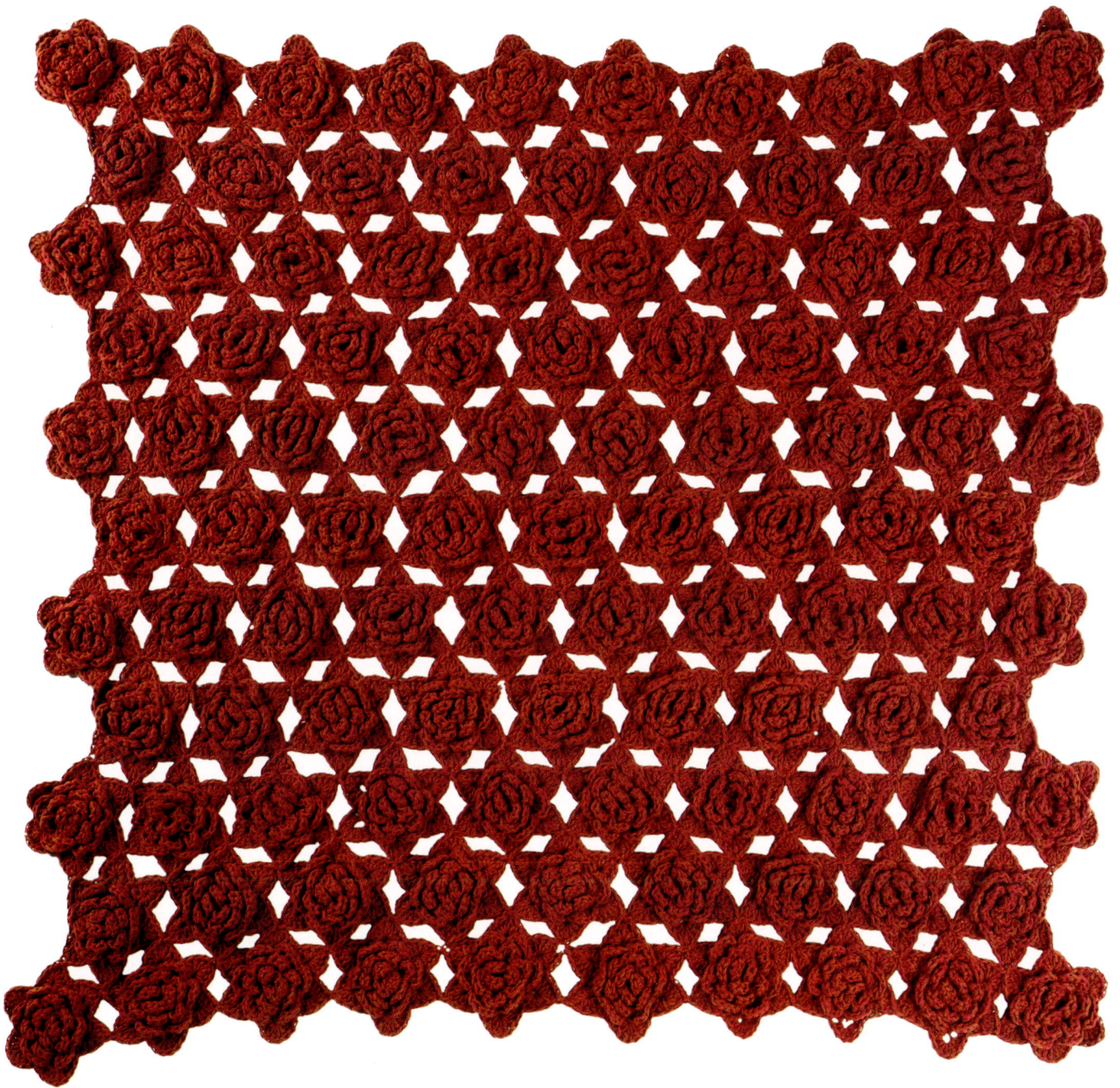

Other Techniques

FOUNDATION CROCHET

The no-chain foundation is an alternate way to start a crochet project. This method is especially useful if your beginning chain and foundation row tends to be too tight. Using the no-chain method eliminates this problem as you are making your chain and the first row at the same time. Because you don't start with a lengthy chain, this method is also very useful when making a large project, such as an afghan.

Foundation Single Crochet

Chain 2. Insert the hook under the top 2 loops of the 2nd chain, yarn over hook, and pull loop through the chain (2 loops on hook), yarn over, pull through 1 loop (2 loops on hook) (1). Yarn over hook, pull through both loops on hook (one loop left on hook), first stitch completed (2). Insert hook under both strands of the foundation chain of the stitch just made (3). Yarn over, pull loop through chain, yarn over, pull through 1 loop (4). Yarn over, pull through both loops on hook (1 loop on hook), second stitch completed (5). Repeat from * for desired length (6). Turn and work the first row after the foundation (7).

Foundation Double Crochet

Chain 3, yarn over, insert hook under 2 strands of 3rd chain from hook, yarn over, pull up a loop, yarn over, pull loop through 1 loop (3 loops on hook) (1). Complete stitch as a normal double crochet (yarn over, pull through 2 loops) twice (2). First stitch made. Yarn over, insert hook under 2 strands of first chain made (3). Yarn over, pull loop through chain, yarn over, pull loop through 1 loop (3 loops on hook) (4). Complete stitch as a normal double crochet (yarn over, pull through 2 loops) twice. Second stitch made (5). Repeat from * for each stitch for desired length (6). Continue rows as regular double crochet (7).

Front Post Double Crochet

This stitch follows a row of double crochet. Chain 3 to turn. Wrap the yarn over the hook. Working from the front, insert the hook from right to left (left to right for left-handed crocheters) under the post of the first double crochet from the previous row and pick up a loop (shown). Wrap the yarn over the hook and complete the stitch as a double crochet.

Back Post Double Crochet

This stitch follows a row of double crochet. Chain 3 to turn. Wrap the yarn over the hook. Working from the back, insert the hook from right to left (left to right for left-handed crocheters) over the post of the first double crochet from the previous row (shown) and pick up a loop. Wrap the yarn over the hook and complete the stitch as a double crochet.

Front Post Treble Crochet

Wrap the yarn over the hook twice. Working from the front, insert the hook from right to left (left to right for left-handed crocheters) under the post of the indicated stitch in the row below (shown) and pick up a loop. Wrap the yarn over the hook and complete the treble crochet stitch as usual.

Seams

There are many ways to join seams in needlework. The ideal seam is flat with no bulk. You can use different kinds of seams in the same garment. Always pin your pieces together before starting to sew.

WRONG SIDE

RIGHT SIDE

Slip-Stitch Seam

The slip-stitch join is a favorite of many because it joins pieces easily. Your stitches must be worked loosely to avoid puckering seams. Place right sides together, draw up a loop 1 stitch from the edge of seam, insert hook in next stitch, and draw up a loop; continue in this manner until seam is completed.

Whipstitch Seam

The whipstitch seam works best for sewing straight-edged seams. Holding right sides together, insert needle from front to back through inside loops, bring through and around, and repeat.

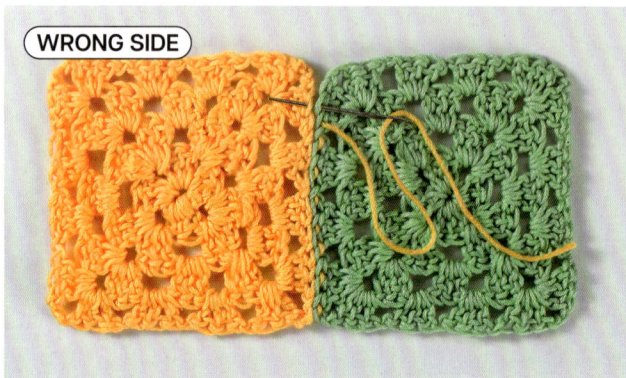

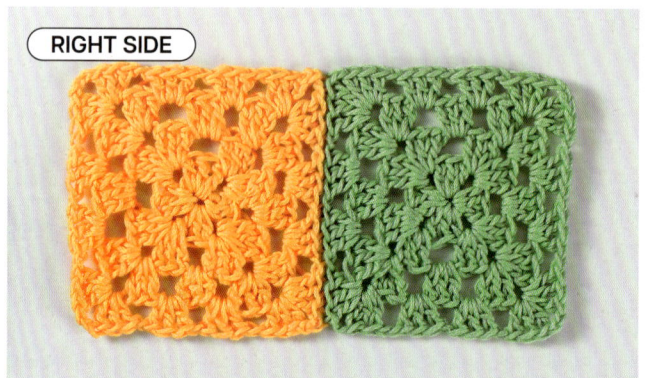

Weave Seam

Hold pieces to be seamed side by side and, working from the wrong side, insert needle from front to back, through 1 loop only, draw through, progress to next stitch, bring needle from back to front (not over), and proceed in this manner until seam is completed. If you draw through top loop only, a decorative ridge will be left on the right side of work. If you draw through bottom loops, the ridge will be inside work.

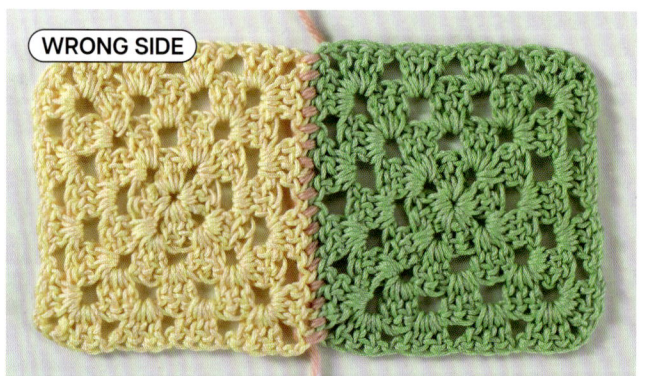

Single Crochet Seam

The single crochet seam creates a decorative ridge; it is especially nice for joining motifs. Holding the pieces, wrong sides together, work single crochet through the whole stitch on both motifs.

Inserting a Zipper

When you insert a zipper into a garment seam, you want the garment edges to close over the zipper teeth, but still allow the zipper to operate freely. Follow these steps for properly inserting a zipper:

1. Baste the garment edges together with a contrasting thread, using the weave seam method.

2. Center the zipper face-down over the seam on the wrong side of the garment. Pin the zipper in place along both sides of the teeth.

3. Using matching thread, hand stitch the zipper to the garment using a running stitch down the center of each side, and then whipstitch the edges. By catching only the inner layer of the crocheted fabric, the zipper insertion will be nearly invisible from the right side. Turn back the tape ends at the top of the zipper and stitch them in place.

4. Remove the basting stitches from the right side.

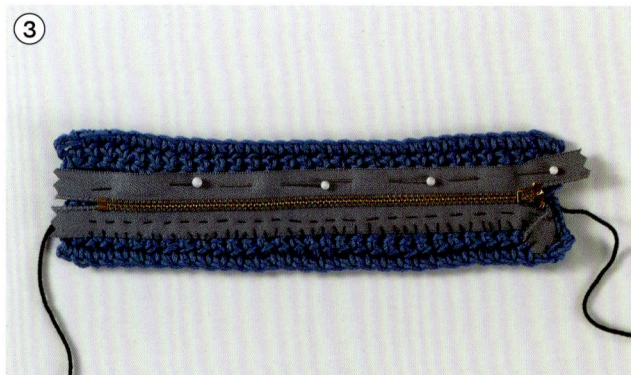

ABOUT THE AUTHOR

Lee Sartori is the crochet designer behind CoCo Crochet Lee. Lee's passion is designing modern, wearable garments and adorable amigurumi. The author of four crochet books, she was formerly a guest host on the popular PBS/CreateTV show *Knit & Crochet Now*, as well as a cast member of Annie's Creative Studio. Lee lives in Halifax, Canada, with her two children, her amazing husband, her adorable bunny, Neville Longbottom, and two cats, Ginny and Toast.

INDEX